Break It Up

Break It Up

Patti Smith's *Horses*
and the remaking of Rock 'n' Roll

MARK PAYTRESS

PORTRAIT

Visit the Portrait website!

· ·

Portrait publishes a wide range of non-fiction, including
biography, history, science, music, popular culture and sport.

Visit our website to:

- read descriptions of our popular titles
- buy our books over the internet
- take advantage of our special offers
- enter our monthly competition
- learn more about your favourite Portrait authors

VISIT OUR WEBSITE AT: www.portraitbooks.com

To Patti Smith, still a True Believer, who, when I put it to her that Horses *was the album that turned the '70s on its head, had this to say just as we were going to press with this book ...*

I have to say that's really nice of you, because when I did *Horses*, I never thought that I would do another album. I wasn't much of a singer, and I certainly wasn't a musician. I did it to inspire other people. My motivation for doing *Horses* was part to thank and remember people like Jimi Hendrix and Jim Morrison, but also to inspire people to take rock'n'roll in their hands and reclaim it. I figured that if people saw my awkward attempts, then they could keep it going. That's always my hope, that people will wake up out of their stupor and do something creative or political, or at least something for themselves.

And to Melpomeni, the most beautiful and thrilling inspiration I could have wished for.

Contents

Acknowledgements

Special thanks to my commissioning editor, Albert DePetrillo, for his continued enthusiasm and last-minute structural fixes; Alison Sturgeon for picture research and editorial duties; Andy Armitage for copy-editing; Karen Langley, a fellow Brian Jones-obsessed teenage Patti fan and a constant source of rare Smith material back in the day; Sara Morrison for transcribing and additional research in my hour of need; Trevor King for fishing out some newly unearthed live material; Julie-Anne Fraser for a few Smith-related loans; Clinton Heylin for coffee and chat; Fred Dellar and Chris Charlesworth; Michelle Przemyck who, on hearing *Horses* for the first time back in 1976, instantly declared, 'I want to marry her!', and, of course, to the fabulous Melpomeni Kermanidou.

Break It Up

Introduction

'I'm not doing this for the glory of fighting, but to change a lot of things.'
Muhammad Ali, 1975

THIS IS NOT A PATTI SMITH BIOGRAPHY. There have been several of those published already, each giving a full account of her life and work, often drawing on original interview material. This book does neither. It is, above all, a piece of polemic. I came of age just prior to the release of *Horses*, and experienced its sea-changing effects first-hand. Having written a small handful of rock biographies, I wanted to exhume the idea, now dismissed as quaint and faintly preposterous, that rock'n'roll had – has? – the power to change lives.

Today, the cultural landscape is far more eclectic and complicated than it was back in 1975. There are probably more artists, more rebels and more to rebel against than ever before. But the artists take the money, the 'rebels' simply walk the walk, and the things that need changing appear indistinct and insurmountable. Guitars and fighting talk seem woefully inadequate. The US government now uses rock music – blasted out at ear-splitting volume – as a weapon against its enemies. That pretty much wraps the whole thing up. But one thing's for sure. *Horses* – opening line: 'Jesus died for somebody's sins but not mine' – is unlikely to suffer that ignominy, which must come as some relief to its peace-chasing maker.

* * *

Meriting ecstatic, full-page reviews on its release in November 1975, and generating at least as much hate-filled bile, Patti Smith's *Horses* was the record that turned the seventies on its head. A *Sgt. Pepper* for the pre-punk generation, though significantly more controversial, it signalled the arrival of an entirely new aesthetic that, within months, had altered the course of rock music and the wider culture for ever.

The record's reverberations were felt way beyond the voguish New York cult art-rock scene from which it sprang. An astonishing fusion of roughly hewn garage rock and stream-of-consciousness poetry, of pop sensibility and avant-garde daring, *Horses* extended the boundaries of the permissible. Representing an unholy alliance of the Rolling Stones and Arthur Rimbaud, of street-level trash and shaman-like artistry, it was a bolt from the gutter that shot towards the stars.

Horses anticipated, encapsulated, *precipitated* a crisis in late seventies rock culture and the arts in general. This book asks why, and how, and takes a closer look at the forces that helped shape it. It is a journey that takes in the primal energy of vintage rock'n'roll, the belligerent sexuality of the early Stones, mid-sixties Dylan nonchalantly opening the gateway of possibilities, the wilful deviance of the Velvet Underground and the riotous, small-town amateurism of US garage punk.

It goes way beyond rock, too, to *belle époque* Paris and the muses of Modigliani, to Père Lachaise and the tombs of the great and the good, to Andy Warhol's Factory and his shooting at the hands of an enraged feminist, to transcendence-seeking poets and trashy underground theatre productions. And, of course, explains why Eric Clapton's favourite colour was red – at least for one day.

There is Smith's own backwater-town upbringing, too, and how pop, poetry and painting rescued her from sickness, solitude and the tedium of academic study. Above all, there is her unflinching belief in the artist as shaman/outsider, which provides the key to her own breakthrough.

That all this erupted so spectacularly around one woman, one record, also owes something to the vacuum that existed in mid-seventies rock culture. It was the era of progressive and hard rock, of acid comedown, soft-shoe sounds from cosy California, of a growing tendency towards rock-as-spectacle. By the mid-seventies rock's radical heart and intoxicated mind had been virtually consigned to the scrapheap.

Things had all looked so different a decade earlier. Then, pop and its young, increasingly freethinking audience were on the cusp of a dramatic cultural shift that promised to revolutionise everyday life. The harbinger of change was no longer seditious, secretly distributed manuscripts such as Martin Luther's 95 Theses or the Declaration of the Rights of Man. The bulletins boomed out from crackly transistor radios and box-shaped record players, from black-and-white television sets and gaily painted discothèques. 'My Generation', '(I Can't Get No) Satisfaction', 'It's My Life', 'Set Me Free', 'I'm Alive' – every second hit single seemed to carry the news. 'How does it feel?' enquired Dylan's 'Like a Rolling Stone', perhaps the key transitional text in the beat era's adoption of beatnik values. Well, during that gloriously expectant autumn, as 1965 turned to face the second, cataclysmic half of the decade, it felt pretty damn good.

By 1975, all the optimism of the second-generation rock'n'rollers had dissipated. The storming of the Bastille, Swinging Sixties style, had given way to the inevitable Reign of Terror. The once young voices of liberation had grown up, grown tired and grown cynical. Dylan's *Blood on the Tracks* might still be regarded as his first mature masterpiece, but, to younger, more impatient and dissident ears, 'Idiot Wind' sounded like a bitter old man singing about himself. Lennon had gone the other way. Having faced his personal demons, and tried a spot of political activism, he'd embarked upon a second spell of adolescence, hanging out in LA with rock's A-list drinking club and knocking out a set of vintage rock'n'roll covers. Jagger, whose lean hips and generous lips once symbolised an entire generation's insatiable appetite for change, was more chameleon-like than the lot of them. His voice now a gruesome parody of that of his younger self, he'd taken to riding a huge inflatable penis on stage and yelling, in air-punching style, 'It's only rock'n'roll – but *I like it, like it, yes I do*!' In the space of half a dozen records, His Satanic Majesty had become a rock'n'roll circus act.

Here she comes . . .
Patti Smith, a saviour of sorts, who refused to accept that it was now *only* rock'n'roll. To her, rock was still a potent force for self-expression, liberation even. Its incorporation into the mainstream entertainment industry was by no means irreversible. From a dark corner in New York, she restated the case for rock as a subversive, subterranean art form.

Here she comes . . .
Horses, a sonic blast of futures and pasts, of street-poet myths, monologues and improvisation, of slurred, Rock-as-Salvation hyperbole.

Here she comes . . .
The Look, dressed down and sexually ambiguous, a model of defiance in stark monochrome.

Here she comes . . .
the first face of third-generation rock'n'roll.

Part 1. Fallen Idols

1. The Big Match

It is 1975. Rock music and its attendant culture has lost its way. A scene develops in the underground clubs of New York that threatens to halt the malaise. From it springs Patti Smith and *Horses*, hailed in some quarters as the most remarkable debut album since pop's sixties heyday. But not everyone is delighted. A bitter battle for the heart and soul of rock'n'roll begins.

RARELY HAS a long-playing rock'n'roll record inspired such delicious delirium and aroused so much ire. *Horses* was 'an album in a thousand' or 'just plain bad', its maker 'the first credible rock shaman' or a 'joker ... celebrating the cult of incompetence'. You were either with it or against it; no fence was in sight.

Though few would realise it at the time, the noisy commotion that accompanied its release heralded a significant watershed in rock and popular culture. The calendar was marked 1975, but it could so easily have been 1789, 1917, 1776 ...

And the words of William Wordsworth, writing about the last days of the *ancien régime*, echoed down the ages:
'Bliss it was in that dawn to be alive
But to be young was very heaven!'

Before *Horses* ...
We wore our hair long and wavy, feigned stoned, beatific grins, decorated our frayed, faded denims with Stars and Stripes peace-sign patches, tottered awkwardly on platform shoes, smoked Moroccan Black, smelled of patchouli, sat down to 'dig' our music, meandering suites of sound that rambled on for 20 minutes (or one side of an LP), played with exquisite grace by public-school-educated Mozarts, their trousers too tight, their mastery of technique exhibited with detached arrogance.

After *Horses* ...
We wore our hair short, dyed and spiky, feigned alienated, angry grimaces, decorated our anything-but-blue-denim trousers with tears and scrawls, loitered menacingly in lace-up boots, drank beer, smelled of solvents, pogoed to our music, furious, fast blasts of noise that never lasted longer than three minutes (or one side of a 45), banged out with untrained abandon by state-school-educated misfits, their trousers too tight, their ignorance of technique exhibited with sarcastic dishonour.

That, at least in terms of subcultural style, is how *Horses* transformed the slow-burn seventies. A lost generation of idlers, depressed and directionless, were given back their youth, their imagination, and the power to transform their own lives. Rock music, for so long in retreat, began to mean something again. And that something was happening *now*.

To insist that *Horses* alone was responsible for the death of dullness, that Smith was the sole midwife to punk rock, is to stretch the point to magazine-cover incredulity. But *Horses* certainly upended a barrel-load of set-in-stone aesthetic principles, and, in so doing, transformed a dead-end decade into one open to all kinds of possibilities.

It was hardly going to be a smooth transition. Such was the impact of Smith's crude, rude, rock'n'roll eruption that *Horses* incited a virtual civil war among the rock cognoscenti. Those who refused to salute her as a saviour regarded her as one of the Devil's own, a crow-headed menace from the underworld on a mission to extinguish the sacred torch lit in mid-fifties Memphis, Tennessee, and latterly illuminating opera houses and sports stadiums. Many viewed that long, strange trip as confirmation of rock's cultural worth, echoing cinema's passage from fleapit to arts faculty. Some, though, dismissed this glittering cloak of newfound respectability as a travesty of all that rock'n'roll stood for.

While *Horses* was a very American record, and Smith herself a rebel patriot in the tradition of Marlon Brando and Jane Fonda, it was in Britain that the ensuing debate for the true meaning of rock'n'roll raged hardest. There, it was possible to find *Rolling Stone* in the racks if you wanted to, but, being colour, prohibitively expensive and as likely to feature Lily Tomlin, Loggins and Messina or Linda Ronstadt on its cover as it was Dylan, Townshend or Jagger, the magazine – a sluggish bi-weekly – seemed to exist only to confirm the utter pointlessness of contemporary (mainly American) rock. Its writers became almost famous simply because the acts they were sent to cover were so damn dull. Can't buy a thrill, indeed. No bite, no bile, not even any beautiful losers. Only that courteous request from the Doobie Brothers – and what kind of name was that? – that we 'listen to the music'. No one thought to ask why.

The London-based inkies, five titles published weekly because rock was still regarded as a matter of urgency on that side of the Atlantic, had been a little more resistant to the contemporary malaise, particularly at *New Musical Express* (*NME*), where Nick Kent and Charles Shaar Murray would routinely champion the damned and debauched antihero (more often from rock's back pages), while lamenting the fact that pop's headline-making edginess had probably gone for ever.

It was Murray who in July 1975 first alerted the magazine's readers to the swelling subterranean scene centred on a small club in downtown New York called CBGB. Two acts particularly excited him: Television, who 'represent[ed] an *imaginative* return to basics', and Patti Smith. 'She knocked me flat on my ass,' he enthused.

It was probably the first time a grown man had been upended at a rock concert since Woodstock in 1969 – and that was only because torrential rain had turned Yasgur's farm into swamp city.

Unlike her fellow neophytes, a fairly static quartet who looked pretty and played more sweetly still, Patti Smith *moved*. More unusual still in those energy-starved times, she could move a crowd. 'She can generate more intensity with a single movement of one hand than most rock performers can produce in an entire set,' Murray insisted. 'She stands there machine-gunning out her lines, singing a bit and talking a bit, in total control.'

Her look, too, was distinctive enough to merit a detailed head-to-toe inspection: '... an odd little waif figure in a grubby black suit and black satin shirt, so skinny that her clothes hang baggy all over her, with chopped-off black hair and a face like Keith Richards's kid sister ...' This was no Suzi Quatro, let alone some cowgirl next door like Tanya Tucker.

Smith's set reached a climax with what Murray called 'an inspired juxtaposition of Land Of 1,000 Dances with a rock-poem about a kid getting beaten up in a locker room'. It was, he concluded, 'undoubtedly the most gripping performance that I've seen by a white act since the last time I saw The Who'.

Which, of course, may have been six months or a decade ago. The point was that the writer, who had come of age when rock was still considered a potent weapon in the West's cultural revolution, had experienced a rare and unexpected disordering of the senses. It's true: watching the Eagles could trigger a similarly altered state, but that was more commonly called sleep.

Both Murray and Kent had continued to fête rock's hip squad of mavericks and misfits – cult heroes such as Syd Barrett, Brian Wilson, the MC5 and Iggy Pop. This was rock's Casualty Corp, beautiful losers who had been indelibly scarred by their courageous attempts to live through their art. Given the potential consequences, it had been years since rock musicians aspired to take an Icarus flight into the Great Unknown. The dark stuff was now negotiated through the prism of vaudevillian charade.

It was Alice Cooper tearing the limbs off baby dolls, cavorting with a snake, getting himself executed, then being chauffeured back to his hotel room, where he'd watch TV and demolish a crate of Bud. Perhaps he was mad, but he certainly wasn't bad or dangerous to know. Or particularly concerned with anything other than being an entertainer, a kind of Bob Hope horror show for the post-Manson generation. Murray's epiphany, which came just as the Carpenters and disco threatened to swallow up rock'n'roll completely, had come as a complete surprise.

But could Patti Smith do it on record? Little over six months later, Charles Shaar Murray had the answer. In what's arguably the most memorable review of a rock record ever, his page-long exposition, published in the 22 November 1975 issue under the headline WEIRD SCENES INSIDE GASOLINE ALLEY, was accompanied by a sensational shot of Smith, fag in hand, and fanlike in her cherished Keith Richards T-shirt. The writer pulled no punches. Significantly better than long-playing debuts by the Beatles, the Stones, Dylan and, more recently, Roxy

Music, he reckoned, and on a par with the first Doors, Who, Hendrix and Velvet Underground albums. Careful only to draw parallels only with super-legends and cult heroes, Murray had copped Bowie's glory-by-association scam (Dylan, Warhol, Iggy, Lou for starters), and had hyped Smith into instant godhead status. A backlash was inevitable.

Chief among the doubters was Steve Lake from *Melody Maker*. With its background in jazz, and a thriving classified-ad section aimed at musicians, *NME*'s more sober rival tended to take its music more seriously. Lake too had seen Smith in concert, but he'd found her performance 'laughable'. His review, published in the 13 December issue of the magazine, was every bit as damming as Murray's had been exuberant.

Unsurprisingly, perhaps, Lake's main beef was with the record's apparent lack of musicianship. Describing Smith and her band as the latest in a long, tawdry line of Velvet Underground wannabes, he complained that, while producer (and former Velvets viola player) John Cale had succeeded in making oddballs such as the Stooges and Nico sound like musicians, he was really 'battling against the odds this time'. The singer didn't impress him much either. 'Smith . . . invariably sings flat,' he moaned.

That was only the half of it. *Horses* typified an encroaching phoniness on the music scene. 'Precisely what's wrong with rock'n'roll right now,' he grumbled, 'is that there's too many academics pretending to be cretins, and too many cretins pretending to be academics.' It was, Lake concluded, time to start shooting them down in flames. 'Let Patti Smith and John Cale be the first heads to tumble.'

That didn't duly concern Murray. He acknowledged that the band sounded 'kind of amateurish and off-the-wall at first, as does Smith's singing'. But, he argued, the aura of mild incompetence was a red herring. 'Patti Smith's album hips you to just what's wrong with a lot of the other stuff you've been listening to,' he declared. It was a bold assessment, and remarkably prescient, given later developments.

Lake continued his assassination by comparing Smith and her band unfavourably with her fellow New York 'numbskulls', the Ramones, the Heartbreakers and Talking Heads. All three were more 'honest', he insisted. 'All those guys actually do have IQs in minus figures.' Murray, meanwhile, was in no doubt that the poet-pariah-messiah was capable of holding her own in far more exalted company.

'*Horses* is an album in a thousand,' he insisted. 'It's an important album in terms of what rock can encompass without losing its identity as a musical form.' Though he resisted the word, Murray clearly believed that *Horses* was rock-as-art – 'some kind of definitive essay on the American night as a state of mind, an emergence from the dark undercurrent of American rock that spewed up Jim Morrison, Lou Reed and Dylan's best work'.

Like Smith herself, the record was

strange, askew and flat-out weird ... Neurotic and unhealthy and dank, a message in a bottle sent from some place that you and I have only been to in the worst moments of self-doubting defeated psychosis ... a thrashing exorcism of public and private demons.

Horses, Murray concluded, was the work of

an artist of greater vision than has been seen in rock for far too long ... It's hard to think of any other rock artist of recent years who arrived in the studios to make their first major recording *with their work developed to such a depth and level of maturity* [my italics].

Steve Lake was having none of it.

The drag is, of course, that half-assed critics with no musical sensibilities whatever will drag their volumes of Freud from dusty top shelves and begin to chunder about Oedipal tendencies and bore us all over again like they once did with Jim Morrison and the Doors. I wouldn't mind at all if Patti Smith was a bona fide nut. But she doesn't even have that distinction.

And so the greatest schism in popular music, at least since Jimi Hendrix set fire to his Strat in theatres packed with Walker Brothers fans, was under way.

* * *

Six months later, in a fourth-floor reception room at the Portobello Hotel in Notting Hill, west London, the doubters' champion was sitting face to face with his nemesis. On the wall behind her, someone had pinned up a copy of his *Horses* review, its POET AND A NO-MAN BAND headline hanging in the air like cheap perfume. Needless to say, things hadn't been going at all well. And now the rest of her band had rolled up.

'OK, Lake,' snarled Lenny Kaye, Smith's lanky guitarist, who had sat in for much of the interview. 'You dealt with the intellect already. Now you're gonna have to deal with the muscle.' Though the writer had made no secret of the fact that he regarded the band as 'jokers', something told him that he'd be a fool to hang around any longer – Kaye's observation that the journalist would 'make a big splash down on Portobello Road', perhaps.

The interview had started surprisingly well given the circumstances. Smith, who was in Europe for a short series of dates, began by holding out a hand of conciliation. 'I don't care if you never write an article,' she told him, adding that it was more important for her to understand why he, a 24-year-old rock critic, was so resistant to what she was doing.

She even handed him the first point. 'The album isn't recorded well, I'll grant you that,' Smith admitted. 'It sounds lousy on the radio.' But that didn't make it a bad record. 'It's a document of how it was,' she explained. 'You can call the record fucked up technically. You can call it a piece of shit. I call it a naked record. Naked and exposed. And I really don't feel that I have to defend it.'

The BIG MATCH, which was how *Melody Maker* subsequently billed the piece, was now under way.

The battle lines were clearly stated at the top of the piece. 'I'm taking a stand against the celebration of the cult of incompetence in rock music,' Lake boldly declared. His mission, he added, was to 'challenge the jokers to defend their music'.

'He thinks we stink,' said Smith, who was determined to hear him out before hitting him with her well-honed powers of persuasion.

Lake next waded in with the sucker punch, putting Smith and Kaye's integrity at the centre of his critique. They were educated, he said; worse still, they were journalists. This apparently excluded the pair from their bold rescue mission, their attempt to massage the tired and heavy heart of rock'n'roll back to life.

'I see their stance as entirely manipulative and calculating,' Lake wrote accusingly. 'The only way that punk rock works is when it comes from the heart. It might be dumb, but it has its own integrity.' He then reiterated a point he had first made in his review of *Horses*. There was, he admitted, a clear lineage between sixties garage punk combos, such as the Seeds and the Standells, and the skinny young bucks coming out of mid-seventies New York, such as the Heartbreakers and the Ramones. But neither Patti Smith nor Lenny Kaye could be counted among them. They knew their stuff. How could they be bona fide pinheads?

Kaye took umbrage. As compiler of *Nuggets*, a two-LP set of scowling, mid-sixties garage punk released to cult acclaim in 1972, he had been virtually responsible for introducing the word 'punk' into the rock discourse. 'We're not a punk rock band because we don't have a Farfisa organ, we don't do three-minute singles and we don't do psychedelic lyrics,' he snapped. Kaye knew his stuff, after all. As a rock journalist of several years' standing, he was acutely aware of the dangers of typecasting, especially so when it barely rang true.

Smith, who considered an attack on her art to be an assault on her whole way of being, was incensed. Critics, she said, were entirely at liberty to call her ugly or skinny or pimpled or technically poor. But there was one particular place that merited no scrutiny. 'The only thing that disturbs me is when somebody questions my integrity,' she insisted.

'We are very, very proud of what we can do,' Smith continued. 'No matter how musically inefficient we may be, I believe we still have something that is unique. A very special form of communication that is usually only blessed to . . . the really great jazz musicians . . .'

Lake took a hard gulp.

Smith galloped into hyperdrive. 'Nobody is doing anything new except us!'

The writer, who'd seen Smith perform twice prior to the release of *Horses*, found the claim preposterous. He responded by reciting her set list. 'My Generation'. 'Hey Joe'. 'Land Of 1,000 Dances'. 'Gloria'. 'Time Is On My Side'. 'Pale Blue Eyes'. 'Louie Louie'. 'We're Gonna Have A Real Good Time

Together'. Some obscure song from a long forgotten Swinging Sixties movie. Roughly half of the Patti Smith songbook seemed to consist of cover versions. Where was the originality in that? Smith's raiding of pop's past was, Lake declared, nothing more than a shameless act of grand larceny.

'There's no way that the completely contrived and affected "amateurism" of *Horses* constitutes good rock'n'roll,' he had concluded in his original review of the album back in November 1975. 'That old "so bad it's good" aesthetic has been played to death.'

It was wide of the mark on two counts. Smith's leap back into history had little to do with covers-band thievery. Her relation to pop's past was deep, reverent and specific and a necessary precondition of her attempt to resuscitate and re-energise rock'n'roll. And, while neither Lake nor even perhaps Smith herself yet knew it, the 'so bad it's good' aesthetic that critics had thrown at *Horses* – which was only part of the story, anyway – would soon spread, virus-like, through the entire cultural landscape.

2. It's Only Rock'n'Roll

Visiting rock gravesides. The Rolling Stones slip into parody. Smith grills the stars and is underwhelmed. *Privilege*, a forgotten sixties film. 'Get Back' and the great rock'n'roll retreat. Patti does the dishes.

THE THIRD OF JULY 1974, the fifth anniversary of the death of Rolling Stones guitarist and founder member Brian Jones.

Beside his modest, well-kept grave on the outskirts of Cheltenham, in the heart of England's green and pleasant West Country, a handful of sombre-looking romantics shuffle awkwardly. More arrive, usually in ones and twos, many journeying there from distant parts of the country. One travels all the way from Japan. The sound of gentle psychedelic music plays from a portable cassette machine. One of his ex-girlfriends is here, someone whispers. There she is, in the distance, blonde and willowy (what else?) and talking to a reporter from the *Daily Mirror*.

Visiting the graves of fallen rock stars became a popular

pursuit during the early seventies. It was better than going to see Uriah Heep.

Days after the fifth anniversary of Jones's death, the Rolling Stones released their latest single, 'It's Only Rock'n'Roll (But I Like It)'. 'It drags its heels worse than a senile rhino,' wrote Pete Erskine in his *NME* review. The single confirmed what many had long suspected, that the Stones had slipped into wretched, hopeless parody. The crass title, the complacent message, the languid performance, everything about the record seemed like a cruel trespass on the memory of the fallen idol.

Was it really now *only* rock'n'roll? In an extraordinary interview with *NME*'s Keith Altham in 1967, Jones had predicted that the 'new pop revolution' would lead to a cultural breakthrough in the arts, theatre, film and music. 'Young people are measuring opinion with new yardsticks,' he said, 'and it must mean greater individual freedom of expression. Pop music will have its part to play in all of this.' He questioned censorship, the Vietnam War, the persecution of homosexuals, the illegality of abortion and drugs and the blind acceptance of religion. 'This new generation will do away with all this,' he predicted.

Jones was not alone. Many commentators, from both sides of the moral divide, had expected the imminent arrival of a new, more progressive society, liberated in part by pop music. But, by 1974, those ambitions were as dead as he was. The Stones' latest single, a relative flop by their standards, gleefully celebrated rock'n'roll for its own intrinsic entertainment value, and nothing more. When Jagger stabbed his fingers into the air, accentuating that 'Like it! Like it! Yes I do!' hook like a playground bully poking at the face of the class misfit, it was a taunt to anyone who'd ever imagined that rock'n'roll was capable of achieving something more than pure entertainment.

But you couldn't place the blame for pop's potency drought entirely on the shoulders of Mick 'n' Keef, even if the once angry young satisfaction seeker was now entertaining HRH Princess Margaret, and the World's Most Elegantly Wasted Man cared for little else save for playing reggae and R&B at maximum volume while awaiting his next consignment of Class A contraband. Just as they always had been, the Stones were a perfect barometer for the times. The sixties had dealt them fame, infamy and a hell of a hangover. As the new decade turned, they were still reeling from recent events: one drowned guitarist, one dead 18-year-old, stabbed by a Hell's Angel in front of the stage while the band played at Altamont Speedway in December 1969, and one awful financial mess. No wonder they now wanted to keep things simple.

Writing for *Fusion* magazine at the start of the seventies, a young rock journalist named Lenny Kaye noted a significant change in rock's sense of ambition, complaining,

> We seem to have run out of steam. 1969 has seen us going through the motions, all form without much substance. We've been left in a strange kind of limbo, where things that once seemed real are no longer, where we have stopped short, waiting for someone to come and take us off into the next stage of the process.

In an early example of the loyalty that later served him so well as Patti Smith's right-hand man, Kaye still placed his faith in the Rolling Stones.

Smith too would find her adolescent attachment to the Stones difficult to give up. They had been responsible for planting the seed of her own personal rebellion, on 2 May 1965, when she unwittingly stumbled on them performing on *The Ed Sullivan Show*. The experience prompted two awakenings, she admitted in one of a handful of pieces she wrote for *Creem* magazine during the seventies: sexual, and 'alchemical'.

By that time, it was clear that rock's sexual revolution had been a success, despite the fact that its stars now tended to look rather drab and undesirable. But those 'alchemical' aspects, by which Smith probably meant anything from spiritual enlightenment to generating social change, had become widely discredited. Only 'nostalgists', acid casualties and communist-supporting, improvised-music mavericks Henry Cow still clung to the belief that popular music had the potential to be anything more than a harmless arm of the entertainment industry.

Despite his enormous and energising influence, Dylan had, after all, always claimed he was nothing more than a song-and-dance man. Jagger and Lennon had both briefly toyed with the idea of becoming rock'n'roll revolutionaries, but soon bailed out when the going got tough. Acid had made the world look as appetising as candyfloss, but once the doors of perception slammed closed again, the aftertaste was doubly bitter.

Patti Smith didn't really do acid, but she found no reason to ditch her belief in the rock'n'roll rebellion. What had worked for her, transforming an isolated misfit into a questioning, creative soul, could work for others too. After her Stones-induced sexual epiphany, Dylan had awakened her to the magical power of language. From there, she discovered art, poetry, sculpture, an entire way of life that spun on the creative urge. But rock'n'roll always remained the king of the sensory pleasures. It informed all her work – the literary homages she penned to her heroes and heroines, the rhythms inherent in her lines (written to the beat of old Rolling Stones songs, she admitted), the plays she wrote, even the way she walked and talked. Smith believed in rock'n'roll, believed it was the most inspirational and sacred art of all. But she, like Lester Bangs at *Creem* (who memorably described the early seventies Stones as 'moneybags revolutionaries'), like Lenny Kaye in New York, like Nick Kent and Charlie Murray in London, despaired at its inglorious retreat. So she decided to do something about it. She sat cross-legged at her typewriter and, with two fingers, started to write.

A brief stint as a staffer for *Rock* magazine proved a profoundly dispiriting experience, as she confirmed to biographer Victor Bockris in 1972. 'I started interviewing people like Rod Stewart, who I admire,' she told him. 'But because of my ego and my faith in my own work, I don't like meeting people on unequal terms ... I couldn't wait to meet Rod Stewart and then when I met him I didn't want to ask him anything.'

She also secured a rare audience with Eric Clapton, by then a largely reclusive figure, exhausted by the musical explorations of Cream and being likened to a deity by aspiring guitar players. Smith began the interview by asking 'God' for his favourite six colours. He saw just one – red. The interview was over. The magazine promptly sacked her, claiming that her work was 'weird'. She soon found her forte, though, writing lengthy, highly personalised piece on sixties bands for *Crawdaddy* and *Creem* magazines. No more interviews, though. 'I figured I'd stop doing that and would wait until they discovered me,' she told Bockris.

The way Smith saw it, the best minds of the rock generation had been cruelly silenced, and for good reason. 'We were dangerous,' she told *Sounds'* Sandy Robertson, who between 1976 and 1978 published several issues of a Smith-zine, *White Stuff.* 'We got snuffed out.' Rock had been too important, she claimed, for the authorities not to notice. 'Who can say how our rock'n'roll leaders died? Drugs . . .?' She tailed off, remembering the four Js – Jones, Jimi, Janis and Jimbo – whom she'd often invoke in her work or in interviews. 'A very odd coincidence,' she continued, 'but it is true that our political leaders were overtly assassinated and there was some conspiracy to push us all down.'

The idea that the transformative, perhaps even revolutionary, potential of rock music and its attendant culture had been deliberately snuffed out was a fairly commonly held belief in the early seventies. The peacenik activities of John Lennon had certainly earned the ex-Beatle a sizeable FBI dossier, though the more usual rite of passage for rock'n'roll miscreants was persecution through (often trumped-up) dope charges. Only in rare instances, as with MC5 manager and White Panther activist John Sinclair (who helped set up *Creem* magazine), and the high-profile Stones busts during 1967 and 1968, were jail sentences deemed appropriate.

It was certainly true that the persistent hounding of Brian Jones had sapped his enthusiasm for the imminent arrival of the new Aquarian Age and contributed to his early death. Hendrix, too. He'd survey the huge festival gatherings of rock'n'roll gypsies and could see the straight world visibly melting away. But he'd not reckoned with the pressures of the business.

The deaths of several of its leading idealists hardly helped the cause. Neither did the shocking case of the homicidal Manson Family, which provided conservative forces with a convenient stick to discredit the counterculture. By 1970, pop's promised land was looking more like a mirage. People no longer talked about My Generation. They had become the Beaten Generation.

That pop's all-conquering energies might actually rebound on those it sought to liberate was controversially forecast in a flop film made at the height of Swinging Sixties optimism. Titled *Privilege*, this British-made movie starring singer Paul Jones and model Jean Shrimpton, two of Carnaby Street's most perfectly formed faces, is a mini-masterpiece of dire acting and *cinéma vérité* artfulness. Its director was Peter Watkins, a thorn in the side of the establishment, whose previous work, the all too believable post-nuclear scenario, *The War Game*, had been sinisterly suppressed. Turning his attentions to what at the time was regarded as the seemingly trivial world of pop, Watkins emerged with an exposé that was hardly less apocalyptic. His thesis suggested that, far from bringing down the establishment, this beat-driven, star-powered arm of the culture industries could be turned against those it aspired to liberate.

The plot centred on pop saviour Steven Shorter, played by Jones, a bona fide mid-sixties pin-up and, until shortly before shooting, the face of Manfred Mann. As the film begins, we see Shorter on stage at the climax of his act. He is manhandled onto the stage in handcuffs, bundled into a cage and ruthlessly set upon by security guards. A brightly illuminated cross glows menacingly at the front of the stage. A mysterious backing band dressed in monks' habits begins to play. Enveloping the entire spectacle is a huge screen that magnifies every nuance in the antihero's agonised countenance.

The song Shorter sings is a pained, despairing plea titled 'Free Me'. The crowd, whipped into a frenzy by the pitiless spectacle, bay for the authorities' blood. The hysteria is scary enough. More sinister still, it is revealed, as the film unravels, that Shorter owes his success to a nefarious, ideologically charged alliance of the church, the state and the corporations. Ostensibly the voice of protest, Shorter is a patsy, an unwitting mouthpiece for the forces of oppression.

His audiences are soon chanting 'We must conform!' But when Shorter's official photographer (played by Shrimpton) gives him a few behind-the-scenes lessons in consciousness raising, he rebels. Alarmed, his sponsors withdraw their poisonous patronage and his adoring fan base turns against him.

Privilege was a crude, and at the time unfashionable, indictment of the pop process. But, from the vantage point of the early seventies, when pop radicalism had slipped, almost unnoticed, from the cultural agenda, it began to make rather more sense.

The film's message was profoundly disturbing, particularly to those who believed wholly in pop's positive energy. But its basic premise – that popular music is a key site for cultural warfare and was therefore worth fighting for – left a deep and abiding impression. Patti Smith was so moved by the film that she reworked Shorter's anthem of mock liberation into her early sets, retitling it 'Privilege (Set Me Free)'.

The more distant the hopes and dreams of the previous decade grew, the more fixated Smith became with saving rock'n'roll. In a summit meeting with ageing beat writer and arch conspiracy theorist William Burroughs in March 1979, she told him, 'When I entered rock'n'roll, I entered into it in a political sort of way. I felt that rock'n'roll, after the death of a lot of the sixties people, and after the disillusionment of a lot of people after the sixties and the early seventies, people really just wanted to be left alone for a little while.' They were, she told him, recharging. 'But when '73 came around, and early '74, it was just getting worse and worse, and there was no indication of anything new, of anyone regathering their strength and coming back to do anything. I felt that it was important for some of us that had a lot of strength to initiate some new energy.'

She laid a similar rap on *Sounds'* Jane Suck, writing for *White Stuff* a year earlier. Her main motivation was 'to inspire', she said. 'I felt that nobody really cared about inspiring the new generations . . . I'd look at them and think, who's gonna inspire them as the Stones did for me?'

The Eagles sure as hell weren't going to.

All was not lost. Just as North Vietnam's rice-growing peasantry had, by 1975, made a laughing stock of the world's greatest military might – a triumph of righteous indignation and outmoded weaponry over indulgent whim and high-tech firepower – Smith and that small pocket of rock-as-salvation evangelists had not entirely given up the fight. It hardly mattered that what they were fighting for was no clearer than it had been a decade earlier. The point was not to give up.

* * *

Pop's state of permanent revolution, epitomised by the Beatles' magnificent metamorphosis from light entertainment goons into psychedelic gurus, was undoubtedly short-lived. Just months after they'd opened the doors to a new cultural paradise with 'Strawberry Fields Forever', three minutes that altered the perceptions of everyone who heard it, they'd closed the lid on 1967's Summer of Love with the unashamedly revivalist 'Lady Madonna'. Fun, and faintly nostalgic for what

soon became known as the golden era of rock'n'roll, it was a
sure step back from the abyss of sonic uncertainty. The record
reinstated them at the top of the pop charts – 'Strawberry
Fields' had been their first 45 not to reach Number 1 since
'Please Please Me' stalled at Number 2 in 1963 – and in some
ways paved the way for Bill Haley to come out of retirement
and lead a fifties rock'n'roll revival during 1968.

Soon everyone was at it. The Beatles followed up with the
even more 'goldie'-sounding 'Get Back' and 'The Ballad of
John and Yoko'. New acts such as Humble Pie, Ten Years
After and Creedence Clearwater Revival based their work on
12-bar rock'n'roll. Gold-lamé-wrapped vocal group Sha Na
Na brought fifties flash to the flooded fields of Woodstock.

Meanwhile, an emerging wave of new-fangled cock
rockers, from Led Zeppelin to Grand Funk Railroad via Foghat
and Savoy Brown, predicated their sound on pumped-up blues
rock. Hairy, heavy and hugely popular, they formed the
backbone for a fast-solidifying rock culture that was to
dominate the early seventies. Priding itself as the antithesis of
pop, rock was in many ways at least as predictable and
apolitical as the 'disposable' pop it looked down upon. Only
now, audiences showered its stars with joints, not jellybeans.

The unfettered freedoms of psychedelic rock, probing its
way towards new sonic spaces and, perhaps, new ways of
living, had proved impossible to sustain. Jimi had jammed his
way into a creative cul-de-sac, his towering musical
imagination overwhelmed by the surfeit of possibilities. Jimbo,
glass habitually half-empty, declared the music over and turned

out the light. And, quitting her fiercely ramshackle band of acid-rock gypsies at the behest of her record company, Janis formed a half-assed boogie unit, before bowing out for good just weeks after Hendrix had done.

Patti Smith refused to join in. She'd been living the rock'n'roll life vicariously, through her idols, and was determined that the hopes she'd pinned on them would not die. So she disappeared into domesticity. Figuring that people needed time to take in the events of the previous decade, she quit her intermittent appearances on the New York underground theatre scene, found herself an aspiring rock'n'roll star of a boyfriend in Allen Lanier, who played guitar and keyboards with Blue Öyster Cult, and retreated so that she might 'find herself'. It was a very sixties thing to do and quite out of character with the prevailing, Warhol-induced New York art-scene aesthetic, which denied everything but the reality of the façade.

Smith was hurt, hurt that her heroes had reneged on their promises, hurt that the Trojan Horse of popular music had been unmasked as a horse with no aim. 'I just got screwed up, so I went into hiding,' she later admitted. She kept shrines to her old idols in the flat she shared with Lanier, on West Twenty-third Street, maintained silent vigils on key anniversaries (usually deaths) of her heroes, and threw herself into the part of a rock'n'roll 'old lady'. 'I was really trying to be a woman for this guy,' she admitted later, adding that she was delighted to remain 'faithful and honourable and also wash his socks …'.

In the great outdoors, beyond the bedroom, the sink and the local launderette, Patti Smith's beloved rock'n'roll was further evaporating into insignificance. Dylan's dive into country rock after his 1966 motorcycle accident had precipitated a mass exodus towards the safety of a musical tradition that stretched way back, long before the invention of the pop 45. More crucially, it marked a key ideological shift, away from the pressing concerns of youth, politics and contemporary activism, and towards an idealised, atomised existence that celebrated individual, not community, acoustic, not electric, yesterday, not tomorrow. An indistinct smog of browns, beiges and blues replaced the gaudy colours of sixties pop and rock fashions. Out went the indiscretions of youthful excess. In came multi-album deals and career paths planned with military precision.

'By the early seventies,' Smith reminded Simon Reynolds in 2005, 'the new artists coming through were very materialistic and Hollywood, not so engaged in communication.' If bands weren't prancing around in cowboy hats, if troubadours weren't soothing the broken hearts and minds of grown-up flower children, they were bragging about the size of their equipment (both mechanical and fleshy), their instrumental prowess and their groupie following. 'As a citizen, I was deeply concerned about what was happening to my genre,' she added.

* * *

'So flower power didn't work, so let's try something new,' bawled John Lennon, speaking at a Free John Sinclair rally in Ann Arbor, in December 1971. But, in terms of ideas, there was very little that was new in rock culture, and nothing seemed to be working. The era of San Francisco acid guru Augustus Owsley Stanley III had gone. Now David Geffen, who directed the careers of Crosby, Stills, Nash & Young, America, the Eagles, Jackson Browne and Joni Mitchell, had the lion's share of influence over the rock narcotic. Sleepy-time time.

Even the airwaves, once the unofficial ministry of propaganda for youth culture, had closed ranks. 'The radio was like the fifties again,' Smith said. 'The alternative radio that we had built up in the sixties was becoming very business-oriented, and programmed like a glorified Top 40. There was no centralised communication ground for the youth of the future, no sense of unity ...'

That was not Smith's idea of rock'n'roll at all.

3. High on Rebellion

The revolutionary power of rock'n'roll. Patti wets her knickers, dances the Monkey, grabs Brian Jones's ankle and becomes a hero-worshipper. The allure of the rock'n'roll iconoclast.

THERE IS A LINE in *Cowboy Mouth*, the play Patti Smith wrote with Sam Shepard, that goes, 'The rock'n'roll star in his highest state of grace will be the new saviour.'

Written in 1971, just as what she called her 'genre' was showing definite signs of fatigue, the aphorism sums up Smith's belief in the redemptive power of the music and its most outspoken heroes that had soundtracked her life. Such is – and remains – her belief in rock'n'roll that you could easily fill a pocket book with her thoughts on the subject.

Recalling her childhood to *Melody Maker*'s Chris Brazier in 1978, she said,

> I was nobody, a skinny little runt that used to hang out, a lot of people's [idea of a] joke, but I had a dream. And my dream was ... to help perpetuate the future of

rock'n'roll into the 21st century. And when I awaken from that dream, I expect to leave behind thousands and thousands of kids quietly sleeping, dreaming the same dream.

Just as rock'n'roll cried out for Patti Smith in the mid-seventies, Patti Smith needed rock'n'roll from the moment she first heard it.

Addressing a boisterous press conference in London in October 1976, she attempted to silence her hecklers with a defiant explanation of why it meant so much to her. 'When I was a kid in New Jersey, there was nothin' happening there, man,' she railed. 'Nothin'. Square dances were all there was. They didn't have any rock concerts or nothin', no cool people or no artists. The only communication I had was rock'n'roll magazines. That was all. It made me feel great. It made me feel less lonely . . .'

Her mother's Maria Callas records, which moved and soothed the young Patti through a series of childhood illnesses, alleviated her pain by bringing beauty into her life. Briefly, she imagined herself as an opera singer, though she got no further than singing a lullaby by Verdi in a school production.

It was the flamboyant and furiously paced 'Tutti Frutti', a January 1956 hit for the strikingly vulgar and Vaselined Little Richard, that first turned her on. For years, Smith had insisted the song had been 'The Girl Can't Help It' (a title infinitely more suited to her persona), before she eventually corrected herself. 'It was instant recognition,' she told *NME*'s Lisa Robinson. 'It really got me below the belt.' The experience seems to have disordered her sense of chronology, too. 'Little Richard got my mind at six and I felt the desire to live,' she enthused, recalling the maroon-coloured Speciality label that spun wildly on her friend's RCA Victrola record player. She couldn't have been less than 10.

Alive to the nascent world of rock'n'roll and the feelings it was able to summon up within her, Smith soon began demanding records of her own – Jerry Lewis's 'Rock-a-Bye Your Baby With A Dixie Melody', Les Paul and Mary Ford's 'Come Josephine On Your Flying Machine' ('the first drug song,' she reckoned), Neil Sedaka's 'Climb Up', even Harry Belafonte's blissfully oceanic 'Shrimp Boats'.

Music for Smith wasn't simply a plastic commodity inscribed with dreams, desires and a dance beat. Inextricably associated with bedridden bouts, it was blessed with healing powers. 'My mother always got me great records when I was sick,' she remembered. Music was as melioristic as it was magnificent. Years later, in a self-penned press biography, she maintained that, 'Rock'n'roll is the highest form of expression since the lost tongue.' It was not hyperbole. She meant every word of it.

Reviewing the Velvet Underground's posthumous *1969 The Velvet Underground Live* double set for *Creem* magazine in September 1974, Patti Smith seemed to be back in her bed, absorbing every passing sound into her sickly body.

There's nowhere higher while youre [*sic*] still in the body physical than to embrace the moment beautiful stranger. Fuck the future man the moment you are reading this is real. Performing is pain is pure ecstatic cut with adrenaline paranoia and any white light one can shoot on stage.

Her alienation caused her to identify with the black kids in her neighbourhood, in Pitman, New Jersey, 'a real spade area', she told Penny Green for Andy Warhol's *Interview* in 1973. And it was Smith's discovery of more exclusively black music that introduced her to the art of performance. Some time around 1963, while at high school, she joined a jazz club, dated a black youth and took a trip to the nearest metropolis, Philadelphia, to see John Coltrane in concert. It was a dramatic, though short-lived experience. She caught just 15 minutes of his set before being ejected from the club for being underage.

While instinctively drawn into the realm of the esoteric, she also found the insistent, commercial beat and satin-like voices lately coming out of Detroit hopelessly irresistible. Coltrane had fed her head, instilling in her the foggy notion of becoming 'a jazz poet'. Motown, the so-called Sound of Young America, inspired Smith to express herself physically.

'I was a great dancer in high school,' she told *Record Mirror*'s Robin Katz around the time of the release of *Horses*. Reckoning she could still mimic every Marvelettes move ('I got all their hand gestures down'), she insisted it was her perfection of the early sixties' dance crazes that gave her the idea for 'a lot of the stage motions I use now . . . boxing gestures in little space'.

She danced the Monkey to Ben E. King at the Philadelphia Airport Drive-In, marvelled at the spectacle of Little Stevie Wonder being carried on stage by the 'Spanish Harlem' hit maker, and did the hand jive along to Smokey Robinson and the Miracles' 'Mickey's Monkey'. 'I didn't like white music,' she told Katz. 'It was either John Coltrane or Smokey Robinson. We didn't have no time for the Beach Boys or the Beatles.' All that changed early one Sunday evening in mid-1965, when she clapped eyes on Mick Jagger for the first time. 'Then I was happy to be white,' she said. 'There was nothing like him.'

It was 2 May, shortly after the Easter vacation. A boy had recently drowned in a nearby swamp and Smith's mother had just returned from the wake. From the television room, her father – an atheist – was shouting 'Jesus Christ!' at the screen. Recalling the moment in orgiastic detail as part of a lengthy piece written for the January 1973 issue of *Creem*, 'Jag-ahr of the Jungle', Smith remembered running into the room panting. 'I was scared silly,' she wrote. And then *it* happened.

'Five white boys sexy as any spade ... in six minutes five lusty images gave me my first glob of gooie in my virgin panties.' They were the Rolling Stones, a surly, arrogant R&B quintet from across the Atlantic. And they had just taken Patti Smith across several critical thresholds – sexual, musical, racial and 'alchemical'. Her life would never be the same again.

Mr Grant Smith killed the television, leaving his daughter blushing, and the damp memory of 'The Last Time' still electrifying her body. (She always insisted it was 'Time Is On

41

My Side', but records indicate they played that only on their first *Ed Sullivan* appearance, in October 1964.) 'But he was too late,' she continued. 'Blind love for my father was the first thing I sacrificed to Mick Jagger.'

Once she'd seen the Rolling Stones, pop for Patti Smith was forever holy and heretic, disorienting and decadent. They were, she told DD Faye, editor of *Back Door Man* magazine, 'like all those adjectives: dangerous, dirty, bad, ugly, disgusting ... wonderful ...'.

Each new Rolling Stones record – '(I Can't Get No) Satisfaction', 'Get Off Of My Cloud', '19th Nervous Breakdown', 'Paint It Black' – sounded like a private love letter, crammed with difficult thoughts, and all the more intriguing for it. Even the hard, misogynist sentiments ('Under My Thumb', 'Stupid Girl', 'Doncha Bother Me') that underpinned the band's 1966 album, *Aftermath*, didn't stop her from devouring it. More than anything, it was that slurred, ersatz American voice of Jagger's that did it, awakening Smith to her own anxieties. That he seemed to revel in his state of alienation only heightened the effect. The Rolling Stones provided a solution – whether it was real or imaginary didn't really matter – to her life.

On Saturday, 6 November 1965, six months after her small-screen sexperience, Patti Smith saw the Stones at the Convention Hall in Philadelphia. It was a half-hour set at most, a mixture of recent hits and up-tempo crowd pleasers such as Chuck Berry's 'Around and Around' and the rhythmic frenzy of 'I'm Alright'. Finding herself caught in the crush down at the front, she reached out for Brian Jones's ankle to save herself, catching his eye as she did so. 'He smiled,' she told Sonic Youth's Thurston Moore. '*He just smiled at me.*'

Patti Smith had become a hero worshipper. 'I felt the people I could learn from were the rock'n'roll stars,' she later told Victor Bockris. 'In the sixties it was Jim Morrison, Smokey Robinson, Bob Dylan, the Rolling Stones. I can still get excited about Humphrey Bogart. I like people who're bigger than me.' And then she said it again. 'I'm a hero worshipper.'

Smith's rock heroes were invariably male, like Jagger, irresistibly, sometimes strangely beautiful, and blessed with near-mythological meaning. They were full-blooded romantic ideals, unafraid to venture to the outer boundaries of experience in a bid to discover, and perhaps even transcend, their true natures. They were the new aesthetes, working at the rough face of a freshly exposed art form. Doing something, saying something, to the whole world – they were *alive*.

The rise and rise of pop opened up new avenues of fulfilment for a previously disenfranchised generation. And no one's voice spoke more loudly, or more freely, during the mid-sixties than Bob Dylan's. By 1965, he had upset virtually every convention going, becoming the most influential man in pop. He ran intellectual rings round Lennon, caused Brian Jones to blow his harmonica so hard that his mouth bled in a bid to impress him, and everyone rushed to cover his songs. All Patti Smith could do was listen, marvel at his visual panache and, well, imagine.

Whether he told it straight or told it ambiguously, Dylan 'had America in the grip of his fist', Smith later recalled. Pretty much everywhere else, too. In awakening pop to the power of the word, Dylan broadened its scope immeasurably. Music could mess with the head or change the world. Anything was possible. When, on 'Positively Fourth Street', he railed, 'I wish that for just one time you could stand inside my shoes,' Patti Smith took him at his word. Dylan was, she knew, the best mind of her generation. She would begin to cast herself in his image.

Dylan's disappearing act after his motorcycle accident in 1966 could have been calamitous for pop had it not been for the emergence of a new kind of rebel romantic in 1967, the year of acid rock and anti-establishment unrest. Doors frontman Jim Morrison, an incendiary cocktail of Jagger-like sexuality and Dylan's poetic vision, was, she told Lisa Robinson in 1975, 'probably the closest to being an artist within rock'n'roll'. Reviewing *An American Prayer* in 1979, a flawed project that set the dead singer's stream-of-consciousness monologues to new, AOR musical backings, she insisted that, 'In biblical times [Morrison] may have appeared as Moses or Samson or his pick of mad prophets.'

Even Smith wasn't exactly sure where the genius of Jimi Hendrix fitted in. 'I don't know what [he] was,' she told Robinson, before locating her iconographer's map. 'He was like some prophet madman, like a rock'n'roll [Antonin] Artaud, because he had some kind of demon within him. He was trying to express it, or find a form for it, but it just swallowed him up like it did Artaud.' (Artaud was a visionary French poet, dramatist and actor, whose dedication to the destruction of bourgeois art forms met with little success and a premature death in an asylum.)

Although most of her heroes died young, Smith was reluctant to admit that their slim grip on life had any bearing on her admiration. 'I didn't love Jimi Hendrix because he died,' she told William Burroughs in 1979. 'I loved what he did when he was most alive.'

By summer 1971, Jones, Hendrix and Morrison were all dead. In the absence of any new alchemists to replace them, the power of the old gods grew with each passing year. Smith's self-belief was developing, too, and, by the middle of the decade, she was beginning to see herself as the carrier of their tradition. 'Hendrix had the process and Morrison had the words,' she told the UK *Daily Telegraph*'s Gordon Burn, 'but neither one had the whole formula. So, you know, I just tried to take it from there.'

* * *

The catalyst for Smith's metamorphosis from obsessive rock fan to obsessive rock performer came when the Rolling Stones, now ripened old objects of desire, sashayed into New York's Madison Square Garden on 25 July 1972. It was, as Smith would have no doubt noted, the night before Jagger's 29th birthday. More pertinently, it was the penultimate date of a vast, energy-sapping US tour, and the singer was, she later recalled, 'on the brink of collapse, the kind of collapse that transcends into magic'. This 'cosmic monkey . . . his face full of silly grace' was so tired he could hardly sing. That night, she insisted, he was 'closer to a poet than he ever has been'.

Fashioning transcendence from utter exhaustion, Jagger – performing in front of a huge mirror that magnified the magic – was, cooed Smith in 1973, 'the total performer, the millionaire martyr'. Her epiphany was total. 'I got so excited I could hardly stand being in my skin,' she remarked some time later, 'and that's given me faith to keep going.' Her experience echoed that of Baudelaire after the poet observed Wagner conducting excerpts from his operas *Tannhäuser* and *Lohengrin* in Paris in 1860. In a letter to the composer, he likened the occasion to, 'a truly sensual voluptuousness as letting myself be penetrated'. Smith, still in domestic seclusion as rock continued to rest in awkward peace, aimed her enthusiasm in an entirely different direction. 'I saw almost a complete future of poetry,' she said. 'I really saw it, I really felt it.'

That was because one name is still missing from the self-styled iconographer's wall of fame: Arthur Rimbaud, prophet, alchemical poet, and the nineteenth century's most enduring antihero. Before the realisation dawned that rock'n'roll was there for the saving, and that she was in a position to do so, Patti Smith had spent much of her late teenage years saving herself from the drudgery of an artless life. And no one nourished her difficult passage from adolescent loner to nascent rock'n'roll queen more than the man often regarded as the prototype for rock's live-fast/fuck-with-art/die-young cult.

4. A Whole Other Reality

Grave spotting in Paris. The death of Brian Jones. God is in the house. The girl looks at Modigliani. Reads Rimbaud. Writes poetry. Works in a piss factory. Has a baby.

IN MAY 1969, Patti Smith quit her till job at Scribner's bookstore in New York and took a plane to Paris. Her mission was to find the ghost of Arthur Rimbaud, the 'mad angel' who'd been her constant companion for the past three years, since she'd chanced upon a paperback edition of his poetry during a lunch break from her vacation job in a toy factory.

When she returned three months later, her head was 'filled with words and rhythms'. Her long-held ambition of becoming an artist's muse, or even an artist in her own right, subsided. She began to write voraciously. With Rimbaud as her ghostly mentor, and the Paris experience giving her a more confident perspective on life in New York, Patti Smith no longer saw herself in the creative gutter gazing up at the hierarchy. Unshackled, she was now 'a tough, dirty Rimbaudian', who was at last beginning to find her literary voice.

With her head filled with the romance of life, Smith had long regarded Paris as a place of worship. For centuries a haven for artists and intellectuals, it was the cradle of existentialism, the capital of *haute couture*, synonymous with stylish cafés, cigarette smoke and conversation, with radical thought and revolutionary action. It was the city of lights, where radicals from Robespierre to Cohn-Bendit had sought to spark dramatic social change, where Modigliani painted his rake-thin muses, and where Gertrude Stein found herself 'all alone with English and myself'. It was where Hemingway, Joyce and Beckett found solace during the interwar years, where modernism and the avant-garde burned most brightly, where Henry Miller and William Burroughs were able to publish their scandalous writings without fear of censorship. It was the home of new wave cinema, where Anna Karina waltzed with coquettish abandon through a series of brain-teasing Jean-Luc Godard movies. And, just 12 months earlier, it was once again the focus of youth unrest, when an alliance of students and workers rioted under slogans such as BE REASONABLE: DEMAND THE IMPOSSIBLE! The city of the Seine was also a haven for the culturally insane.

Paris wasn't simply a place where great dreams were played out. 'So this is where people come to live,' wrote Rilke in 1910. 'I would have thought it a city to die in.' Many poets and painters took him at his word, and Patti Smith scoured the labyrinthine Père Lachaise cemetery for the tombs of her dead heroes, visiting as many as she could. She got closer still to the ghost of Arthur Rimbaud, by managing to book into the attic room at the Hotel of Strangers, where the poet once lay with his lover Charles Cros.

According to Smith, she also spent five days there repeatedly watching Godard's latest film, *One Plus One*, which included footage of the Rolling Stones working on 'Sympathy For The Devil'. If true, then it's certainly a testament to the city's voyeuristic effect on her. But, despite the observational overload, she failed to find herself as an artist during her Parisian sojourn. 'I always felt that I was in a black-and-white 16mm film,' she told Penny Green in 1973. 'Paris to me is completely a city of images. I found it impossible to work there.'

Instead, she hung around with a fire eater, Adrillias, and his motley crew of circus-style entertainers, some of whom introduced her to the gentle art of pickpocketing (justified, no doubt, by Robert Bresson's film *Pickpocket* and Jean Genet's *A Thief's Journal*). She dressed in black – 'In Paris, everyone's a poseur,' she said later – and passed herself off as a transatlantic Edith Piaf.

One morning, she purchased an English music weekly and was shocked by the news that Brian Jones was leaving the Rolling Stones. The recurring image of Jones, so obviously the lonely Stone in *One Plus One*, conspired with the headline to haunt her dreams. 'It was always water,' she remembered: Brian in the rain, Brian floating, Brian's head in the toilet.

One night in late June 1969, Smith scalded herself with boiling water. It prompted another visitation. This time, Smith and Jones were being pulled perilously into a whirlpool. She knew it: something was about to happen. Days later, the newspaper headlines confirmed her fatal clairvoyance: BRIAN JONES MORT.

When she began to have similarly dread-filled dreams of her father, she freaked out, packed her bags and hotfooted it home. Back in Pitman, Grant Smith was laid up in bed. He'd suffered a heart attack. Paris, it seemed, was also the city of nightmares.

The mind of Patti Smith had always worked overtime. 'I was a little loose in the attic' was how she later explained it to *Rolling Stone*'s Dave Marsh. A string of childhood illnesses, including tuberculosis and scarlet fever, prompted a series of intense hallucinations.

Born on 30 December 1946, Patricia Lee Smith was the baby boomer who was too busy living in her head to appreciate fully the newfound comforts of postwar American life. Not that there was too much of that in her household.

'I was a little girl in New Jersey,' she said in a late seventies interview for Japanese television. 'I was a very sick little girl and skinny. They didn't even know if I would live. We had no money, we were very poor, and my brother and sister were in hospital with malnutrition.' So she'd simply lie down and let her 'mind spill out', never once imagining that things would always be that way. Belief was, after all, a potent force in the Smith household.

Her father, Grant Smith, a tall, handsome man with a vaguely comic air about him, wore his trousers high and Brylcreemed his hair. He worked night shifts in a local factory in Pitman, a backwater town deep in The Pines, a swamp region in a pig-farming southern part of New Jersey. Having started out on Chicago's south side, the family had relocated there in 1955 in search of the good life, via a sheep farm in Tennessee and a spell in Philadelphia. One of the major employers in the area was Columbia Records, who owned a pressing plant there.

To the eight-year-old Patti, her father, a 'Deep Purple'-whistling atheist who read the Bible and books on physics and UFOs, was 'equal parts God and Hagar the Spaceman'. He was, she maintained, something of 'an intellectual'. Her mother, Beverly, who worked in drugstores and waitressed in order to supplement the family income, was 'like a real hip Scheherazade'. Between the two of them, she told Dave Marsh in 1976, Smith 'developed a sensibility'.

Extricating reality from projection and fantasy isn't always easy when getting to grips with Patti Smith's early years. Her father was, she has said many times, a tap dancer. Her mother's alternative career was as a jazz singer with a 'cigarette tenor' voice. Both were more likely ad hoc sidelines. Music, though, was ever present.

What prevailed above all was a persistent struggle between conflicting faiths. Her father encouraged his four children – Linda, Todd and Kimberly had all come along by 1959 – to blaspheme and 'swear against God'. But her mother, who erred towards religious fanaticism, tended to hold the cards. Young Patti absorbed the icons and rituals of Catholicism, and soon grew to love all the most colourful characters, especially Cain,

Eve and Lucifer. As a young teenager, she would accompany her mother on often fruitless attempts to offload piles of the Jehovah's Witness newspaper. The family were never into 'goody-goody interpretations of the Bible', Smith later insisted. But it's no surprise either to learn that prayer-happy Patti once harboured a desire to become a missionary.

It's quite possible that Beverly Smith, like the mother in Jeanette Winterson's *Oranges Are Not the Only Fruit*, projected the baby Jesus on her firstborn: '*You* can change the world.' What's almost certainly true is that the Smiths inhabited a world filled with heathens and demons with 'unnatural passions'. As with the proverbial Hollywood baddie, it was almost inevitable that these would soon acquire a forbidden kind of cachet.

Patti Smith, a self-confessed, and perhaps self-loathing 'ugly duckling', found it easy to relate to the bad guys. Scarlet fever had made her hair fall out. She had a lazy eye, too, one that 'used to go up in my head', she later told Lisa Robinson. 'It was creepy-looking. So I had this eye patch. I was about ten pounds, had duck feet and glasses.' If they weren't already teasing her, her classmates would demonise her as 'Winghead', a name derived from the peculiar way her hair stuck out at the sides.

'I never got to be the fucking swan,' complained Cavale, the character Smith played in *Cowboy Mouth*. 'I paid all those dues and I never got to be the fucking swan.' Plain, weird-looking and ostracised, the black swan had little option but to retreat into her own private fantasy world.

'When I was a little kid I always knew that I had some special kind of thing inside me,' she told Victor Bockris. 'I mean, I wasn't very attractive. I wasn't very verbal. I wasn't very smart in school.' Her end-of-term reports often stated that 'Patti Lee daydreams too much'. Her quest to bag herself a bad boy, one of those brooding characters who carried switchblades in their tight black trousers, was also doomed to failure. 'But I had this tremendous hope all the time,' she added, 'this tremendous spirit that kept me going no matter how fucked up I was.'

Slowly, surely, Patti Smith came to understand her acute outsider status as a gift. Eventually, this self-confessed 'sort of a weirdo' discovered that she wasn't entirely alone. There was a place that misfits could call home. 'My real world wasn't so hot as a kid,' she told *Sounds'* Stephen Demorest in 1978. 'Art gave me a whole other reality.' She continued:

> Art totally freed me. I was skinny and awkward, but one day I found Modigliani, I discovered Picasso's Blue Period, and I thought, Look at this, these are the great masters, and the women are built like I am. I started ripping pictures out of the books [and no doubt Modigliani's 1917 painting, *Draped Nude*, was one of them] and taking them home to pose in front of the mirror.

It became an obsession. Twenty years later, she insisted that she could still adopt 'almost any Modigliani pose'.

There was no freedom in art in Jesus' world, Smith learned through her Jehovah's Witnesses teachings. But the discovery that so many of the great masters – from El Greco to Jackson Pollock and his 'jazzy dance steps' – found beauty in a female form not dissimilar to her own enabled her 'to create an entirely new self-image and make it seem acceptable'. Modigliani's models were especially influential. 'They had long thin necks, pale faces and solemn expressions,' Smith said. She could have been describing herself on the cover of *Horses*.

No longer able to commune with God, Patti Smith instead adopted artists – as well as pop musicians – as saints and seers, especially those who had an eye for women cast in her own image. Of course it was narcissism, but it was also an essential first step in gaining some sense of self-worth.

For an art-fixated teenager who burned with missionary zeal, there was one obvious career trajectory. So in autumn 1964, at the age of 17, Smith secured a scholarship to Glassboro State Teachers' College. Her desire was to open the eyes of her students in a way that hers had been opened. One lecturer, Dr Paul Flick, took her to one side and talked to her about the social function of art. 'He really got it through me that criminals were often failed artists, like Hitler wanting to be a painter,' she told Stephen Demorest. The good doctor instilled in her the idea that art was a 'transformation of energy' that helped to relieve psychic tensions.

Rock'n'roll had awakened Smith to the physical side of the creative urge. Painting was subtler, more cerebral, and encouraged her to regard herself as a living work of art. Literature soon completed the triumvirate, closing the circle of aestheticism that shielded Smith from the humdrum realities of the day job, and the artless chatter of those who blindly accepted it. Inured from the fear and loathing of the outside world, she embarked upon a life of glorious impoverishment, immersing herself in the life of the romantic outsider that enabled her to detach herself, perhaps even discover new truths about herself, and about the crooked, constipated energies that ruled the world.

Her first taste of this as a young adult came in 1966 when she took a vacation job doing piecework at the Dennis Mitchell Toy Factory in Woodbury, South Jersey. Between long shifts spent inspecting baby-buggy bumper beepers, cutting straps for pushchairs and assembling cardboard boxes for baby-sized mattresses, she was mercilessly ridiculed by her fellow workers, at one point even having her head plunged down an unflushed lavatory bowl. 'Twenty years of schooling and they put you on the day shift,' Dylan railed accusingly on his 1965 hit, 'Subterranean Homesick Blues'. Smith knew just what he meant.

For a young woman who preferred to dress in dark clothes and hide behind shades – 'My Greta Garbo period,' she said later – hanging out at the Philadelphia Museum of Art offered a welcome respite. She didn't exactly feel comfortable among the largely Jewish art crowd, dressed in their black leotards and zooming off in their brand-new sports cars, but at least she wasn't persecuted for her passions. It was there that she first encountered Andy Warhol and his 'Superstar' protégé Edie Sedgwick, in town for the opening of his first retrospective.

Right across the rail track from where she worked, in a small bookshop where she'd seek refuge during her lunch breaks from the factory, she picked up a cheap paperback. It was a bilingual edition of *Illuminations*, Arthur Rimbaud's prose-poetry masterpiece, written in the early 1870s on a diet of absinthe and other mind-altering stimuli, at the height of his affair with Paul Verlaine. Fuelled by dreams and hallucinations, *Illuminations* was the manifestation of Rimbaud's desire to risk his own sanity in order to uncover the unknown. It was his greatest achievement in his quest for what he called *dérèglement*, popularly translated as 'the derangement of the senses', that state of mind that enabled him to break through to the 'alchemical' other side.

Smith has recounted this first 'meeting' with Rimbaud on numerous occasions, and for good reason. It is probably the most significant of all her heroic encounters, for it provided her with a largely unsung genius she could call her own, and a philosophy of art that she later adopted in her early approach to rock'n'roll.

Rimbaud, who also grew up in a strongly religious household, sought nothing less than truth through transcendence, utilising dream states and mysticism in his quest to lift the veil of the material world. In 1871, when just 16 years of age, he wrote his famous *Lettre Du Voyant*, a manifesto in which he delineated an entirely new approach to art and life. In it, he denounced his predecessors, argued in favour of 'new ideas and forms' to replace order and convention, declared that poetic truth was necessarily dangerous, and that only a *voyant*, a seer, could penetrate the true meaning of self and things. Unusually, he was also an advocate of the feminine consciousness, declaring that, 'When the unending servitude of women is broken . . . she will discover things strange and unfathomable, repulsive and delicious.'

It was deliciously heady stuff for the factory-bound Patti Smith, who had picked up the book on the basis of the jacket. 'There's that grainy picture of Rimbaud and I thought he was so neat-looking and I instantly snatched it up,' she told Victor Bockris in 1972. 'I just thought Rimbaud was a neat name . . . I thought he was so cool.' With a full head of long, curly hair, this Dylan lookalike seemed to be roughly a century ahead of his time.

Her colleagues weren't impressed at all, accusing her of having communist sympathies and creating such a commotion that Smith walked out. If truth were told, she didn't understand much of Rimbaud's work either, admitting later that she 'didn't really fall in love with writing as writing. I fell in love with writers' lifestyles.' In the first instance, she got hooked on Rimbaud simply because he was 'a mad angel and all that shit'.

But Patti Smith was hardly illiterate. Her freethinking father had read her H.G. Wells at bedtime; her mother brought a wider range of reading into the home, everything from comics and fairytales to Robert Louis Stevenson's *A Child's Garden of Verses*. Most influential of all was Louisa May Alcott's *Little Women*. Its main character had been 'a really big influence', she later admitted. Jo March was teacher at an all-boys school with literary aspirations. She wrote plays for her pupils to perform, and also indulged her secret self by writing bawdy tales on the side. Strong, tomboyish and yet in touch with her femininity, she was an early role model for the young Patti Smith.

Inspired by Jo March, Smith wrote plays too, and had her siblings dress up and perform them. She also tried her hand at short stories, and by her mid-teens was writing poetry at high school. It was all third-hand stuff, she later admitted, 'about everything I didn't know about . . . I was a virgin. I had never faced death. I had never faced war and pestilence.' It was, nevertheless, a beginning.

While at Glassboro, where she 'failed everything', Smith gravitated towards a small writing circle. Inspired by Rimbaud, his mentor Charles Baudelaire, and, most observably, the Spanish poet and playwright Federico García Lorca, she started to take her writing more seriously. One Lorca-inspired poem, 'Almond Tree', about the rape of a girl by her brother under the pale moon, was, it has been suggested, based on her own experiences at the hands of a stranger. Patti Smith was learning to insert herself into her own work.

In summer 1966, Smith's sexual awakening rudely impacted on her own life when she discovered she was pregnant. Traumatised, she moved out of home and stayed with a hippie-type couple miles from Pitman. 'I was gonna kill myself but I'd have missed the next Stones album,' she quipped later. But the event made a deeper impression than that.

In 'Female', written in April 1967 and published in her first volume of poetry, *Seventh Heaven*, in 1972, she writes about the trauma of being, 'bloated. Pregnant ... like a lame dog', of her desire to pull her 'fat baby belly' to the sea, pull her hair out by the roots, claw 'like a bitch'.

The physical experience hit hard, too. 'One thing that knocks ego out of a woman is childbirth,' she told Stephen Demorest. 'It's the heaviest experience.' The pain was excruciating, she added, and it awakened her to something primeval and to survivalist instincts. 'You become a common denominator with the soil,' she explained, and she was left feeling 'like a wolf'. She did what any lone wolf would do, and ran.

After giving birth in February 1967, Smith gave the baby daughter up for adoption. A supportive teacher at Glassboro organised an escape route by arranging for her to attend a nonexistent course in New York. Further assistance came with the latest Rolling Stones single, 'Let's Spend The Night Together'. 'It's impossible to suffer guilt when you're moving to that song,' she reckoned, evidence again of her looking towards rock'n'roll to provide solutions to her life. She also played Dylan's *Blonde on Blonde* incessantly during her pregnancy.

With experiences piling up around her, Patti Smith could no longer mistake herself for an armchair activist, a dance-floor consumer, a *flâneuse*, an idler who inhabited art galleries and carried a book everywhere. She'd seized upon art to help her understand – and perhaps escape – life. Now she too had something to contribute. 'I gave [the baby] up ... because I wanted to be an artist,' she remembered. 'I wanted to create and recreate in my own way.'

The age of great dreams was certainly on her side. It was spring 1967 and a pungent scent of self-expression hung in the air. The hot, heady Summer of Love was just weeks away. But scour the footnotes of Patti Smith's life and you'll find few references to this extraordinary cultural moment, a time enshrined in 'Papa' John Phillips's harmonious depiction of an entire generation 'in motion'. A determined outsider, Patti Smith was not about to throw out her hands and embrace the collective alienation of the hippie movement. Instead, she identified with the romantic violence of Jimi Hendrix, the destructive urges of Jim Morrison, the fragile, butterfly-like beauty of Brian Jones. To her, flower power smelled of phoniness. And, sure enough, by the autumn, the dark evenings set in, and love no longer seemed adequate to cure the world's ills. Besides, by then she was down and out and living in New York, a city hardly disposed to California sunshine.

5. A City of Work

Meeting Mapplethorpe. Hippie-induced nausea. Trying her hand at sculpture. Brian Jones (again). The Chelsea Hotel. Masturbating in the name of art. Back at Rimbaud's graveside.

NINETEEN SIXTY-SEVEN. Hot town, summer in the city, and Patti Smith was eking out an impecunious existence in New York. The young woman who believed in adventures, but was only just beginning to live them out, had arrived there in late spring – it was the Doors' 'Light My Fire' that prompted the move, she would claim – with just $16 and some basic art materials in her bag.

Many years later, Smith spoke vividly of the ratlike existence of her early days in New York, living on the street and in the subways. In truth, she probably landed a little more softly than that. Within days, she'd found a cashier's job at Brentano's Bookstore on Fifth Avenue, bang in the centre of Manhattan, where another young seeker, aspiring photographer Robert Mapplethorpe, was working part-time while studying at the Pratt Institute of Art in Brooklyn.

She was 19 years old, and, counter to the prevailing 'turn on, tune in, drop out' values of the flower children, she regarded New York as 'a city of work'. Over the next few years, she took a series of jobs, usually in bookshops, where she felt connected to culture and was more likely to meet people who felt the same way.

Meeting Mapplethorpe, an elfin-like George Harrison lookalike who was also 19 and gripped by a similar urge to create, was a remarkable stroke of fortune. The pair soon sensed they were kindred spirits, two dreamers from America's giant suburban sprawl who had come to New York to look for art, liberation and, ultimately, recognition. Smith has described her relationship with Mapplethorpe as 'a chance encounter that would change the course of my life'.

Smith was lonely, traumatised and confused. Mapplethorpe, on the other hand, was merely lonely, and confused only in matters pertaining to his sexuality. Artistically, he was confident, almost precocious. '[He] taught me how to direct my energy,' Smith recalled later. 'I was a victim of intense nervousness ... hallucinations, manic energy, and I didn't know what to do with it.' Mapplethorpe did. Already disciplined in his attitude to work, he encouraged her to unleash the creative soul within, and to pursue her aspirations as an artist.

For the next five years, the pair spent much of their spare time together, sometimes as lovers, often to spur on each other's ambitions. 'I lived a very hermetic life with Robert,' Smith told Stephen Demorest. 'He was the one who [got] me to the point where I could exorcise all the demons in me into good work.' She hit her 'peak period', she stated, between 1969 and 1970.

New York gave Patti Smith the confidence to be herself. 'Everyone thought I was weird [in South Jersey],' she told Penny Green. 'All I was was romantic, not rebellious. No one stared at me here. New York was like a huge cathedral. I could come here and hide. It's the only place that really accepted me.'

Now she was free to be who she wanted to be, her newly unharnessed freedom of expression did not necessarily bring her closer to the mass outpouring of communality then sweeping the youth of the Western world. In a prose piece, 'Flying Saucers Rock'n'Roll', published by *Crawdaddy* magazine in June 1975, she recalled her acute sense of apartness while attending a hippie party at the height of flower power. Jimi Hendrix's debut album, *Are You Experienced*, was playing and all she could feel was a sense of alienation akin to the 'nausea' Sartre described in his 1938 novel of the same title. 'I wasn't in on it,' she wrote. 'I couldn't stand it.' Interestingly, she adds that she was simply 'too plugged into sanguine rhythms past and the silver video we call future' to let herself go. There was something complacent and slavish about the Now that prevented Smith from joining in.

The present times were never enough for Patti Smith. That's why she lionised Rimbaud when everyone else bowed down to the new electric gods; why she walked around the vicinity of the Pratt Institute and imagined she was in Montparnasse during the *belle époque*; why she read books on Modigliani and Romanian-born abstract sculptor Brancusi instead of Tolkien and Heinlein. And why, rather than model herself on Grace Slick, she imagined herself as an artist's mistress. The flat she shared with Mapplethorpe in Hall Street, Brooklyn, in late 1967 and 1968, may have been fashionably decorated with tapestries and beaded curtains, but Smith chose to live, as she famously sang years later, 'in another dimension'.

Settling into her hermetic existence with Mapplethorpe, Patti Smith slowly developed a vision of herself as a creator, thus allowing herself to engage with the contemporary at one remove. With the photographer's constant affirmations, she let go of her desire to become an artist's muse, though not because it was anything less than a noble pursuit. On the contrary, she often asserted, it was a testament to the power of the muse that Modigliani repeatedly painted Jeanne Hébuterne, or that every second Godard movie was a love letter to his wife Anna Karina. Instead, her shift in aspiration had been because she had discovered 'a white tiger clawing to get out' of her, an expression first used by Theatre of Cruelty playwright and certified madman Antonin Artaud. 'I wasn't born to be a spectator,' she insisted years later.

With Mapplethorpe hard at work in the same room, Smith ploughed herself into her work, though her earliest efforts were probably more about exorcism than excellence. Inspired by her reading, she tried her hand at sculpture. 'I wanted to be like Brancusi,' she told Stephen Demorest, 'getting the soul of the rock, but I stank.' Her fine-art training had not prepared her for working in three dimensions, and, besides, she was simply incapable of visualising what she was working towards. 'I loved the tools, and the process of chipping away,' she said, 'but I had no actual image that I was looking for.'

Smith was more successful when she turned her attentions back to drawing, something she soon found herself doing obsessively, for up to four or five hours a day. The page was a repository for her demons, a paper theatre where she'd wrestle with – again from Artaud – her 'tumours'. She wanted them out, these 'pains in my head, double vision. I didn't want to wind up like [Artaud, who died in a lunatic asylum]'. Not for the last time she looked to the Native Americans for inspiration. 'Crazy Horse used to say, if you take my picture, you steal my soul, so I figured I'd take [that is, make] pictures of these demons, and if I got them down perfectly I'd rob them of their power.'

Eventually, probably some time early in 1969, that particular battle was over. Inspired by a scene from *All the Hipsters Go to the Movies*, where two angels, one Muslim, the other Christian, rip each other's entrails out, Smith returned home and recreated it on paper. It was, she said, a moment of catharsis. 'My drawings were all extensions of that struggle,' she told Stephen Demorest, 'and I learned to successfully control it.'

What she couldn't control was Mapplethorpe's sexuality. The pair had been lovers at least for some of their early months together, but after a bust-up with Smith, the photographer took off to San Francisco. On his arrival home, she returned to their shared flat, after a brief liaison with another artist, and discovered that Mapplethorpe had redecorated the place with an assortment of gay images. Shocked and hurt, she packed her bags and moved in with Janet Hamill, an old friend from Glassboro State Teachers' College.

According to Jack Walls, quoted in *Please Kill Me*, Gillian McCain and Legs McNeil's oral history of the New York underground scene, the incident 'broke Patti's heart . . . Before that, the only thing Patti and Robert argued about was who was gonna do the laundry.'

Smith gave up her job at Scribner's bookstore, where she'd spent the past several months 'serving up genius' to customers, and, with her sister Linda in tow, took off to Paris in search of Arthur Rimbaud. She had also reached a creative impasse. 'I thought, fuck art, I want to be a traveller,' she said later.

Returning to the States in July 1969, shortly after the death of Brian Jones, Patti Smith visited her bedridden father before making her way back to New York. After she discovered that Robert Mapplethorpe was struggling with a gum infection, the pair made up and decided to move in together again. Having recently followed in the footsteps of innumerable writers and artists while in Paris, Smith headed off to the Chelsea Hotel, on West Twenty-third Street, where she convinced owner Stanley Bard that the pair were worthy of renting the smallest room in the block, on the 10th floor.

The Chelsea was steeped in history. Dylan Thomas – Bob's

namesake – drank himself into a stupor there. It had been a haven for the Beats; William Burroughs, Allen Ginsberg and Gregory Corso were still regular visitors. So too was Janis Joplin, Jefferson Airplane and various hip rock'n'roll luminaries. It was also the place where, in 1966, Andy Warhol filmed his split-screen, 'Superstar'-filled epic, *Chelsea Girls.*

'The Chelsea opened up a whole new thing for me,' Smith told *NME* in 1975, 'the rock'n'roll thing.' That was true: she now found herself rubbing shoulders with the new rock aristocracy, and establishing relationships with characters from the inner circles of both Warhol (Gerard Malanga) and Bob Dylan (Bobby Neuwirth). Inevitably, some of their magic rubbed off. For the first time in her life, Patti Smith started to see herself as an active player in the wider countercultural community. She conversed with Burroughs, sang to the noted field-recording collector Harry Smith and most significantly, at least in terms of her transition from spectator to spectacle, wooed Malanga with her poetry.

Even when she was playing at being Brancusi, or doing line drawings of her friends and heroes, Patti Smith had never stopped writing. But now, after her callow Rimbaud- and Lorca-inspired efforts back in New Jersey, she'd discovered a new freedom in her writing. She'd started by adding speech bubbles ('balloons' she called them) into her visual frame. 'Then the words get bigger and they obliterate the balloon,' she told Robin Katz in 1975. Words became her 'new hallucination'; phrases began to emerge with their own metre, 'just like train rhythms ... crazy rhythms'. She began to reconsider poetry. 'I would rebel and say, I'm not going to write it. And it started getting louder in my ear. I had to start carrying a notepad with me all the time.'

Writing poetry didn't come any easier to her than sculpture or painting had done. But, since returning from Paris, Smith began to realise it was the art form that suited her best. Soon, her small orange notebook started to fill up, mostly with her attempts to write a requiem for Brian Jones. 'And of course they were rock'n'roll-oriented because they were about Brian,' she said, 'and I would write them in the rhythm of the Stones' music. I wasn't trying to be innovative. I was just doing what I thought was right, and being true to Brian.'

Heroes had always been inspirational to Patti Smith, though it was by no means inevitable that she'd write about them. That dubious honour was usually left to teenage readers of fan magazines. But, in writing about them, she found a focus that had previously been missing, and besides it was the truth. Her earliest drawings had included pencil representations of Rimbaud, Italian poet and film director Pier Paulo Pasolini and Jane Bowles, but they hardly moved with the beat of the times. Poetry was different. Poetry was physical.

Dylan had been – still was in her opinion – a rock'n'roll poet. Patti Smith found a new métier. She could be the poet who rock'n'rolled. She was learning to create the moment. 'It's like pumping blood into words,' she told *NME* in 1975. 'Poets are always anaemic-looking and I just want to pump a lot of blood into it.' On another occasion, she insisted that she wrote, 'with the same fervour as Jackson Pollock used to paint'.

Over in England, a one-hit wonder named David Bowie was about to make a name for himself partly by his conspicuous consumption of the lives, and legends, of others – usually noted renegades such as Andy Warhol, Aleister Crowley, Lou Reed and, of course, Bob Dylan. Patti Smith too began to weave herself into the fabric of stardom via vainglorious association with her heroes. Not everyone was convinced by the method, especially in an era when the worship of anything other than 'hazy cosmic jive' (as Bowie later had it) was regarded as distinctly uncool.

Smith was unfazed. 'I'm not doing it to drop names. I'm doing it to say this is another piece of who I am,' she claimed on more than one occasion. Her heroes were an honest expression of her own desires, perhaps even her own wish fulfilment as she aspired to attain the greatness they embodied. 'I'm not a fame fucker,' she told Victor Bockris in 1972, 'but I am a hero worshipper. I've always been in love with heroes. That's what seduced me into art.'

Taking her cue from Arthur Rimbaud, she started to see herself as a *voyant*, a seer, upsetting the field in order to create something new from it. With few exceptions – notably Allen Ginsberg, who wasn't averse to reading out his work bollock naked while pumping out drones on his harmonium – contemporary poetry was static and sombre. 'Poets have become simps,' she complained, 'the sensitive young man always away in the attic.'

Patti Smith determined to be different. Yes, she was the sensitive young woman in the attic, crafting her work in manic, marathon sessions from the 206 West Twenty-third Street atelier she'd shared with Mapplethorpe since moving out of the Chelsea in spring 1970. But her libido-driven verse had all the verve of a classic mid-sixties Rolling Stones single. It had sex. It had rock'n'roll. But drugs? Smith rarely had need for that. She was, as she often reminded the world when she eventually got the chance, high on rebellion. And, if that failed her, there was always masturbation.

'I don't consider writing a quiet, closet act,' Smith acknowledged later, emphasising its physical aspects. 'When I'm home writing on a typewriter, I go crazy. I move like a monkey. I've wet myself, I've come in my pants writing.' Heroes such as Rimbaud, Genet and Burroughs had all relied on onanistic self-love as an aid to their work – though they'd throw drugs into the mix, too. 'Instead of shooting smack, I masturbate – fourteen times in a row,' Smith boasted. To her, 'fucking and masturbation and art are all the same because they all require total concentration'. All good artists have one hand down their zipper, she once claimed, but women have the better deal. 'They are multi-orgasmic, so they can do it all day,' she told *Circus* magazine's Scott Cohen in 1976.

It is little surprise that Smith's first volume of poetry, *Seventh Heaven*, was rich in sexual desire. What was remarkable was her subject matter: her love interests were almost exclusively women. Although all 22 poems are shot through with the magical spontaneity of Rimbaud, the one-word-sentence economy of Céline and, to a lesser extent, what she called the 'hammer language' of Mickey Spillane, whom she'd discovered more recently, these almost exclusively male influences produced a work of indeterminate sexual orientation. Many quietly assumed that Smith was a lesbian.

'Actually, it was the first time I considered women at all,' Smith told Penny Green several months later. 'But I didn't know how to do it, so I had to do it like I thought myself as a guy. All of these poems are about women, seduced, raped … me in a male role.' On the rare occasion that she did assume a female role, in 'Longing', for example, she was, Smith admitted, 'a complete victim … That poem [inspired by her new-found love for Allen Lanier] … was the first time I considered that a woman's true position was on her back.' After years of denying her potential for passivity, Smith was doing what every true artist does: explore the unthinkable.

Her work made no secret that her admiration for women – including Joan of Arc, Maria Falconetti (the silent-screen siren who played the French saint in Carl Dreyer's 1928 movie classic, *La Passion de Jeanne D'Arc*), Warhol 'Superstar' Edie Sedgwick, Amelia Earhart, Modigliani's mistress Jeanne Hébuterne, Rolling Stones girlfriends Marianne Faithfull and Anita Pallenberg (the latter to whom the volume was co-dedicated) – sometimes spilled over into sexual desire. 'I need a chick,' she stated at the top of 'Girl Trouble', her homage to Pallenberg. 'I'm / ready to fish my fingers in / part that butt / and press against her opening.'

Smith admitted that at least some of her verse had been written 'to seduce a chick', that Pallenberg might read 'Girl Trouble' and invite her to the south of France for 'a little nookie'. But there was something vicarious at work, too, in her celebration of the (mainly) doomed heroines of *Seventh Heaven*. She didn't necessarily want *them*: it was their power, their alchemical allure, that she was after.

* * *

After she'd spent four years on the periphery of cultural activity in New York, things began to change for Patti Smith during 1971. Having established the true nature of her relationship with Robert Mapplethorpe, after which she enjoyed brief liaisons with the playwright Sam Shepard and the singer Todd Rundgren, she met and fell in love with Allen Lanier. A handful of makeshift poetry readings at the Chelsea gave her the confidence to go public, and, with Malanga's patronage, she held her first poetry reading at St Mark's Church in February 1971. The following year, she made a second pilgrimage to Paris, where she underwent another epiphany.

Ostensibly, she'd come to pay her respects to her most recent fallen idol, Jim Morrison, who had died in his bath there the previous July. Some sources suggest he was masturbating and that, unlike that of the woman who was poised to claim his crown, his fatty, tobacco-heavy heart couldn't take the strain. But, as she stared down at his grave, a 'dirt site' in Section Six in the Père Lachaise cemetery, there was no spiritual meeting of souls, no nothing. It was raining, she remembered, writing up the experience for *Creem* in 1975, and all she could think of was a dream she'd once had. Morrison was trapped, his wings having merged with the marble slab as he struggled in vain to free himself. 'He was struggling to get free but like Prometheus freedom was beyond him.' Smith ended her piece with the words, 'We don't look back.' It was as much a statement of personal intent as it was anything else.

She also visited Rimbaud's grave. Again, nothing. She straightened her skirt and made her way back to the hotel. 'Fuck it!' she told herself. 'I'm going home and doing my own work. I'm not standing over the graves of these people.'

Part 2. Rising Star

6. Street Hassle

Warhol gets shot to the beat of a Patti Smith song. Valerie Solanas on why all men are S.C.U.M. New York toughens up. Patti's Ridiculous Theatre. Here come the young men: Malanga, Carroll, Shepard, Rundgren. Hanging out at Max's. The New York Dolls hit the scene.

THIS IS a book about Patti Smith but, as in all the best Jean-Luc Godard movies, there is an indiscriminate shooting that breaks up the narrative.

> *Andy was in the Factory talking on the telephone*
> *At the other end of the line Viva was gossiping*
> *Another girl was waiting in the Factory*
> *She merged perfectly with the Factory*
> *She merged perfectly the mania in the Factory*
> *The girl looked at Andy Andy said 'Don't!'*
> *but the music kept playing as planned*
> *The girl shook Andy she pressed a gun against him*
> *She shot it in she shot it home she shot three deep in Andy*

The girl disappeared Andy fell to the floor
started losing his wig under the table
started losing his wig under the table
started moaning passionately
Then suddenly Andy
Gets the feeling
He's being encircled by
Voices voices voices voices

Whispering ...

'Andy?'

* * *

It's 3 June 1968, and Andy Warhol's not up for ponying or partying or painting or anything else tonight. In fact, he's clinically dead, as dead as his waxy, masklike complexion, now the whitest shade of pale, always looked. Below his still, almost serene face is a meat harvest of body parts, laid bare by the surgeon's scalpel, which has sliced Andy's chest apart. A little later, a doctor massages his heart back to life after its tick-tock stopped for a full 90 seconds.

A single gunshot, fired from a .32 automatic, has brought Warhol to this place, an emergency room in the Columbus Hospital on Nineteenth Street, between Second and Third Avenue. Just a few hours earlier, he'd been browsing in Bloomingdale's, 'gee'-ing and 'wow'-ing and letting his jaw fall slack at everything he saw. He often limbered up for his day job that way, before spending a leisurely afternoon at his Factory studio, watching, listening, exchanging gossip. Now and then, he'd entertain an art dealer or a potential business partner, before the real business of partying began as evening fell.

But today just wasn't Andy's day. That was always going to belong to Valerie Solanas. She'd woken up with the express intention of shooting someone. A man. It had been coming for some time.

Solanas had purchased the gun a few weeks earlier with $50 given to her by Paul Krassner, a small-time publisher of radical tracts. She then told him that she intended to shoot Maurice Girodias, director of the Paris-based Olympia Press. Solanas also had the long, dark raincoat with pockets deep enough to conceal the weapon, and the lipstick and the hair job that did wonders for her otherwise pasty-faced, boyishly plain countenance. ('Doesn't Valerie look good!' were Warhol's first words when he encountered her outside the Factory at 4.15 that afternoon, just moments before the shooting upstairs.) Above all, she had the motive – a mumbo-jumbo jive of militant feminist martyrdom and misunderstood-artist syndrome.

After she turned herself in to police at around eight that evening, Valerie Solanas explained, 'He had too much control of my life.' In fact, Warhol's crime had been blind indifference. An infrequent visitor to the Factory since early 1967, Solanas had appeared briefly in two Warhol movies, *I, A Man* and

Bikeboy. Her real ambition, though, was for the artist-turned-film-producer to shoot a script she'd written, *Up Your Ass.* Warhol had read it, but reckoned it was 'so dirty' that he suspected a police set-up and so promptly forgot about it.

After Maurice Girodias had handed her a $500 contract for a novel earlier in the year, Solanas's persecution complex intensified. She believed the publisher and Warhol were in cahoots to appropriate her work and ideas. In fact, when she left home on the morning of 3 June 1968, Girodias had been her intended victim. She had spent three hours outside the Chelsea Hotel waiting for him to emerge, before finally accepting the concierge's explanation that the publisher was away for the weekend. She took off in the direction of the Factory.

Less than 12 hours later, as she was being brought to book, Solanas greeted a braying pack of reporters with a simple message: 'Read my manifesto!' It was her 'I'm ready for my picture, Mr de Mille' moment.

Solanas had self-published her *S.C.U.M. Manifesto* in 1967 and had managed to sell a handful of copies on the streets of New York. A long and surprisingly erudite, albeit hate-filled rant concerning the oppression of women, it argued for the creation of a Society for Cutting Up Men (hence the viciously amusing acronym) as the only way to remove the eternal bondage of female servitude.

The 21-page manifesto begins thus:

> Life in this society being, at best, an utter bore and no aspect of society being at all relevant to women, there

remains to civic-minded, responsible, thrill-seeking females only to overthrow the government, eliminate the money system, institute complete automation and destroy the male sex.

By the end of her treatise, her vitriol knew no bounds. 'Rational men want to be squashed, stepped on, crushed and crunched,' she raged, 'treated as the curs, the filth that they are, have their repulsiveness confirmed.'

Solanas's rude interjection into the cultural politics of alternative New York was as mood-altering as the drugs everyone seemed to thrive on. The near assassination of one of its own caused a good deal of introspection, even among Warhol's not so Beautiful People. Coming so soon after the assassinations of Martin Luther King and Robert Kennedy, it showed that the creative community was not immune to the grim realities of the modern world.

Many felt there had been an element of karma about the shooting, that the artist's voyeuristic, indifferent attitude towards those who had inveigled their way into his circle had rebounded back on him. While Warhol sat impassively, occasionally picking up his hand-held movie camera to record an otherwise insignificant moment for posterity, or else mumbling some trite piece of gossip into his Dictaphone, the bodies and the minds of the misfits and the fame seekers and the freeloaders around him began to pile up. They were his 'Superstars', their deviant habits and neuroses magnified in grainy, full-screen glory in his low-budget films. To others, such as the underground filmmaker Jona Mekas, they were 'sad, desperate souls', victims of the hideous cult of fame. After Warhol's shooting, the vibe around the Factory inevitably changed, with what the poet Ed Sanders described as 'switchblade types' and 'A[mphetamine]-heads' descending on the place.

By the end of the sixties, much of the paranoia and outrage of the Warhol set had spilled onto the New York stage. And Patti Smith, part Solanas-like outsider theorist, part aspiring Warhol-set fame seeker, was there to help trample the last bloom of the Love Generation into the soil. However, goodwill for plain-faced, rake-thin women was in short supply after the Solanas episode. Smith would need all the help she could find.

The turn of the new decade marked, Smith said later, the period when she 'made the transition from psychotic to serious art student'. And, like all typical art students, she was now willing to give anything a go, especially if it enhanced her own creative self belief. Now that she'd tried her hand as a solitary poet, sculptor and painter, her next step was to cross the threshold from private to public, from lone-wolf pursuits to spotlit exposure in front of an audience.

As her social circle widened, so her skin thickened. When she was asked to appear in the La Mama production of *Femme Fatale*, which came under the umbrella of John Vaccaro's Playhouse of the Ridiculous, she accepted without quite knowing what she was getting into. The 'Ridiculous Theater' crowd was largely made up of Warhol-styled 'stars' from the street who often indulged in high-pitched slanging matches while all dressed up in various shades of glitter. The play took its title from a song by the Velvet Underground, one-time house band at Warhol's Factory. The script was based on the memoirs of the noted NYC speed-freak and transvestite Jackie Curtis, later immortalised in Lou Reed's post-Velvets hit 45, 'Walk On The Wild Side'.

And Patti Smith was invited to play the part of a man, John Christian.

Photographs of Smith from the time are remarkable in that they bear virtually no traces of Woodstock Generation exoticism. Often dressed simply in a man's white shirt and skinny black trousers, her long, thin face framed by hair tousled Keith Richards style, Smith looked every inch the magnificent monochrome street urchin that would turn heads in 1975. Another contemporary shot finds her resembling a boy biker in her favourite Robert Bresson movie, *Au Hasard, Balthazar*, her hair tucked behind her ear, a cigarette hanging from her lips.

Smith thought she looked like a perfect cross between French screen icon Jeanne Moreau and the Rolling Stones' guitarist. Quoted in *Please Kill Me*, Penny Arcade remembers her differently. 'Some people thought Patti was this ugly girl, you know, when ugly was a sin. But she wasn't ugly. It was just that nobody looked like that then. She was really skinny and dressed weird. She had this look that was completely her own ... a precursor of the whole punk thing.'

Jackie Curtis wasn't particularly enamoured of her, bitching to anyone within earshot that she was nothing more than a social climber. Terry Ork, who later went on to manage Smith's New York contemporaries Television, was marginally more generous, reckoning she

> was living a very public persona. Patti would always kiss somebody and then look at you to make sure you'd noticed, almost as if she were acting out a 1920s Paris Bohemian role. She was very self-conscious about living as if she were on stage . . . She had that New York bravado.

He also described her, a little uncharitably, as 'a starfucker'.

Smith returned to the stage playing the part of a speed freak in Tony Ingrassia's production of *Island*. Her role was to stand at the front of the stage commenting – Brecht-like – on the action. The infamous underground transvestite, Wayne County, talked of revolution. Smith faked shooting up while screaming, 'Brian Jones is dead!' at the top of her voice. Needless to say, the production was largely based on improvisation, and Smith used the freedom to broadcast her obsessions.

Offstage, Ork's observation was gaining some credence. Sometime early in 1970, while she was living at the Chelsea, a man in a dark suit and glasses walked in through the lobby. 'I've always been a sucker for guys in dark glasses,' she recalled in 1975. He noticed her and called out, 'Hey, kid, where did you learn to walk like that?' She told him she had perfected her moves from watching *Don't Look Back*, D.A. Pennebaker's documentary of Dylan's 1965 UK tour. The mystery man introduced himself as Bobby Neuwirth, Dylan's aide who had featured prominently in the film. He took her under his wing, and over the next four days introduced her to the hotel's rock'n'roll star residents. Starstruck Smith fell in love. 'He was the last vestige of the sixties cool,' she remembered, and that 'really got me by the heart'. Neuwirth failed to understand the obsession with Brian Jones, but he was impressed by her work, telling her, 'We need a poet.'

Next up was the charismatic and prodigiously gifted poet Jim Carroll. He'd already picked up the Random House Young Writers Award for *The Basketball Diaries,* his memoir of teenage drug addiction. The Nureyev-like Carroll was impoverished, erudite and an expert on the work of New York School poet Frank O'Hara. She was smitten and brought him a coffee, chocolate doughnut and Italian ice-cream breakfast each morning at the Chelsea. By the second half of 1970, Carroll had moved into Smith's loft flat at 206 West Twenty-third Street. Carroll had a model girlfriend. Smith, who still roomed with the now openly gay Robert Mapplethorpe, had no one.

Jim Carroll turned her on to the chatty, informal style of O'Hara, himself not averse to hero worship, as his 'Thinking of James Dean' indicates. He also introduced her to happenings down at St Mark's Church. Located in the East Village in downtown New York, the venue was a popular haunt for the city's poets and artists, where Monday night was open-mike and Wednesday was when the bigger names came to read. It was where Smith would make her first public appearance as a rock'n'roll poet.

Eventually, she came to regard the St Mark's poets as 'namby-pamby', especially after Carroll was banned for not turning up to a performance, despite the fact that he'd been banged up in a prison cell. She regarded Carroll as a genius, a latter-day Rimbaud. 'He is a true poet,' she said many times. 'He's a junkie. He's bisexual. He's been fucked by every male and female genius in America. He's been fucked over by all these people. He lives all over. He lives a disgusting life. Sometimes you have to pull him out of a gutter. He's been in prison. He's a total fuck-up. But what great poet wasn't?'

In terms of lifestyle, the two were opposites, with Carroll remembering that his soulmate in syntax was a kindly, mothering type with an aversion to drugs. In their work, too, Carroll noted a major difference. While he regarded his approach as rational and essentially Apollonian, Smith 'had this whole Dionysian thing ... She could just go nuts and counterpoint with this sweet self, and let go with this weird-angry-magic self, too.'

It was a playwright, however, and not a poet, who entered Patti Smith's life and taught her the most about her craft. Sam Shepard, then in his mid-twenties, was a prolific off-Broadway writer who was rooming at the Chelsea when Smith first met him in autumn 1970. A veteran of several performances in the upstairs theatre at St Mark's, Shepard soon became her soulmate, lover and writing partner. Sharing in her admiration for larger-than-life antiheroes – he specialised in gangsters and cowboys – Shepard was, Smith recalled, 'the most true American man I've ever met'. His entire life 'moved on rhythms'. Shepard wasn't scared to negotiate the worlds of literature and rock music either, and after she'd taken him to see the Stooges, the pair collaborated on a two-person play, *Cowboy Mouth*. She'd lifted the title from one of her favourite Dylan songs, 'Sad-Eyed Lady Of The Lowlands', the lengthy finale of *Blonde on Blonde*.

Written in one marathon all-night session on a single typewriter ('like a battle', Smith told *After Dark*'s Robb Baker in 1974), *Cowboy Mouth* was a stream-of-consciousness dialogue between what Smith called, 'two big dreamers who came together but were destined to come to a sad end'. The play's run lasted no longer than it took to write. After the first night's performance, on 29 April 1971 at the American Place Theatre, Shepard, who was already married, disappeared. What was essentially a public demonstration of an adulterous affair made even this bad boy distinctly uncomfortable. Smith, who appeared under the pseudonym Johnny Guitar (named after the 1953 Nicholas Ray movie starring Joan Crawford), later described the play as 'The true story of Sam and I'.

Cowboy Mouth contained more than a germ of wish fulfilment, at least on Smith's part. Among her lines, which she surely wrote herself, was a monologue that doubled as a manifesto for the emergence of a new rock'n'roll saviour. In the role of Cavale (French for 'escape'), prostrate on an unmade bed and goading Shepard's character Slim into becoming a rock star, she says, 'People want a saint but with a cowboy mouth, somebody they can look up to.' After dismissing her old heroes Bob Dylan and Mick Jagger ('He got too conscious,' she says), Cavale continues to attack the contemporary stasis. 'The old saints don't make it, and God is just too far away. He don't represent our pain no more.'

The stars might have fallen, but Cavale still sticks firmly to her belief in rock'n'roll. 'Any great motherfucker rock'n'-roll song can raise me higher than all of Revelation,' she continues. 'We created rock'n'roll from our own image, it's our child ...'

The old masters had gone out to pasture. After a brief affair with Todd Rundgren, Patti Smith voluntarily joined them. She continued to write during her self-imposed exile. She wrote a poem, 'Star Fever', for the sleeve of Rundgren's 1973 album, *A Wizard, A True Star*, which seems to stick to its subject matter resisting any obvious references to the pair's tryst. She also wrote a couple of lyrics for Blue Öyster Cult, 'Baby Iced Dog' and 'Career Of Evil'. It has also been suggested that she was asked to front her partner's band, but that she turned them down.

Meanwhile, as she lay low for an extended convalescence, the New York underground rock'n'roll scene was going through some dramatic changes, changes that were to lay the foundations for her eventual rebirth as a rock'n'roll performer.

The city's underground scene had a peculiarly twisted take on rock'n'roll long before she-devil Valerie Solanas shot her way into New York folklore and plunged the scene into desperate, get-it-while-you-can decadence. While teams of professional songwriters worked to a handful of templates in the Brill Building across town, two poets, Ed Sanders and Tuli Kupferberg, decided to have a little provocative fun with pop (of sorts) and late in 1964 formed the Fugs. Theatrical, literate and political, their heavily ironic work – one song was titled 'Kill For Peace' – was subject to bans and censorship. The Fugs played underground rock before the phrase was even invented.

The Velvet Underground, who formed shortly afterwards, sounded nothing remotely like the Fugs, but they were similarly unclassifiable – at least until a decade later, when everyone aspired to achieve a 'Velvet Underground sound'. Led by the sexually ambiguous Lou Reed, who spat out his odes to heroin, transvestism and other deviations with deadpan cruelty, the group created high art from the trash can of contemporary culture. But it was their early champion and benefactor Andy Warhol who contributed most to the emergence of a specifically New York cultural aesthetic.

Warhol worshipped celebrity, and the shy boy from Pittsburgh didn't mind whether it came wrapped in old-money furs, or in silver foil from the nearest supermarket. Pop artists, pop stars, rent boys and poor little rich girls – all were welcomed into Warhol's vast culture dome, as long as they brought their battling egos, and any other bad habits, with them. Everyone at the Factory was under the magnifying glass. The result was a menagerie of misfits, each in hot competition with the other, many using aliases in order to draw further attention to themselves.

But worship, of both the brilliant and the banal, was only part of Warhol's contribution to the emerging cultural scene. The man who famously wanted 'carpets in the street' and 'money for everybody' was a one-man revolution in much the same way as Rimbaud was. Turning old-fashioned romanticism on its head, he dealt not with esoteric interior lives and art as lived or imagined experience, but with the reality of the surface. He cultivated the idea of the human being as a machine and replicated this in his work via his technique of the screen print.

The result was probably the most brilliant art-and-life project of the twentieth century. While the arrow of sixties rebellion was aimed at both society and the self, Warhol categorically denied the possibilities of improving either. More voyeur than Rimbaud-like *voyant*, he simply looked and magnified. If there was social critique in his multiple images of icons and disasters, it was an ironic mirror to the death-and celebrity-obsessed world in which he found himself.

Warhol didn't know how to dance – he got lookalike Edie Sedgwick to do that for him – but he did know how to party. In April 1966, he hired an old ballroom, the Dom, for a now-legendary series of events where the Velvet Underground performed at ear-splitting volume, while Gerard Malanga and Mary Woronov danced alongside them with whips and chains. It was profoundly more sinister than the psychedelia-inspired idiot dancing popular in San Francisco, and its effect was to cast long, deep shadows through the New York underground scene.

Unlike its Californian countercultural cousin, where the preferred activity was to let it all hang out, the scene that grew up around Andy Warhol was, in a word, uptight. The drugs – usually speed or smack – were heavier, the egos bigger, and the worldview was subterranean and kinky rather than psyched-out and kaleidoscopic. And Patti Smith wanted in.

By 1970, she was a regular at Max's, the bar-and-restaurant bolthole favoured by the Warhol crowd. Warhol and his cronies had made it their second home since its owner and proprietor Mickey Ruskin first opened its doors in December 1965 – and spent increasingly more time there after his shooting, when the artist became noticeably more cautious about whom he invited to the Factory.

Initially, Patti Smith and Robert Mapplethorpe, she in her street-urchin apparel, he in an array of floppy hats, were left on the steps outside, virtually begging for someone to invite them in. One night, record company A&R man Danny Fields (who'd been largely responsible for bringing the Stooges and the MC5 to Elektra in the late sixties) took pity on 'this adorable, sexy young couple in the doorway' and invited them to share his table. It was at Max's that Patti Smith saw the Velvet Underground, during a low-key 1970 residency towards the end of the band's life.

But, by that time, the Velvets had lost the hyped-up-'n'-trashy electronic sonic aggression of their early career. Their viola-playing bassist and resident noisenik John Cale had left in 1968 after a battle of the egos with frontman Lou Reed, and the band now played at a supper-club pace. The songs were still good, but even Reed felt uneasy trading under false pretences and quit the band shortly afterwards.

The Stooges (fronted by Iggy Pop) and Alice Cooper both passed through Max's and divided audiences with shows that were high on theatrically driven rock'n'roll brutality and low on instrumental prowess. Things might have been different had they come out of New York, but both acts were always associated with Detroit and, though kindred spirits, they were always regarded with suspicion by the flippant fops from the Factory.

Only when a bunch of cross-dressing, streetwise misfits from Manhattan started to flex their exaggerated presences across the stage at the Mercer Arts Center – housed, oddly, in the Broadway Center Hotel in downtown New York – did the city have a band truly to call its own again. Devoid of the Velvet Underground's dilapidated art-house ambition, which they replaced with a gaudy sense of drama that owed much to Theater of the Ridiculous-style outrage, the New York Dolls rattled out glammed-up, three-minute rock'n'roll to an audience comprising both young street kids and Warhol 'Superstars'. Lead singer David Johansen took his cues from Jagger; guitarist Johnny Thunders and the mob-handed musicians beside him got their stack heels imported from England; and the city's rock scene once again had a focus for its legendary bad attitude.

Distilling rock'n'roll down to its basic elements – sex, simplicity and an unquenchable desire to show off – the New York Dolls were archetypal. Their seventeen-week Tuesday-night residency in the 200-capacity Oscar Wilde Room, where mirrors magnified the group's faggy appearance, began on 13 June 1972. No one was quite sure whether the band were the best they'd ever seen or the worst. But they reignited the New York underground, attracting the attentions of Lou Reed, the London music press and even Warhol himself.

By the start of 1973, the Dolls had played London, where drummer Billy Murcia died of a drugs overdose, managed to wind up Mick Jagger, who was less than flattered by Johansen's wholesale appropriation of his act, and succeeded in securing a record deal. Back at the Mercer, as they waited to take the stage for another night of Pills, Bad Girl, Jet Boy and the distinctly Warholian Personality Crisis, a young woman was reading a poem about surrendering herself to Arthur Rimbaud. Patti Smith was about to cross over into rock'n'roll.

7. I Want the World and I Want It Now!

The first public poetry reading. Lenny Kaye, Nuggets and garage punk. Billy Graham and Adolf Hitler. Patti finds her own rhythm. The first concert.

ON THE NIGHT of 12 February 1971, as Patti Smith walked off the small stage at the St Mark's Church Poetry Project, she began to cry. She had just finished her first public performance and was both elated and emotional. The applause that still rang in her ears made her feel, she remembered later, 'like Gloria Swanson'. For the past 15 years, she'd been on the other side of the performer–audience divide, cheerleading the entertainers who had brought her hope and inspiration. Now, all the acclaim was hers. She had read some words, she had laid bare her passions and obsessions, and she had held an audience. It was 20 minutes that shook her world. Patti Smith was now a bona fide performer.

In truth, not everyone who was there that night had welcomed her with open arms. She'd turned up with a guitarist for a start, which was hardly going to endear her to poetry purists. While her demeanour – wiry, edgy, tomboyish – was only mildly out of step with the usual acts, her delivery was dramatically different. She swayed in rhythm to her stanzas, and punched the air to emphasise key words. It was hardly the performance of a bedroom bard, facing the unrelenting glare of the spotlight for the first time. According to eyewitness Victor Bockris, Smith 'had the confidence and courage to machine-gun her poems at the sophisticated if slightly stunned crowd'. On hearing a recording of the performance taped by rock manager Steve Paul, journalist Dave Marsh reckoned that, 'in her voice were not simply references but the very rhythms of rock'n'roll'.

Smith had been invited to perform by Gerard Malanga, who headlined that night. Thanks to his long-time role as Warhol's assistant at the Factory, the audience was well connected, with Lou Reed and Andreas Brown, owner of the Gotham Book Mart, among those attending. Heavyweight, though determinedly outré, literary references framed her performance.

It was the birthday of the German communist playwright Bertolt Brecht, so Smith – whose diary was filled with notable dates – began with a version of 'Mack The Knife', one of the playwright's Berlin theatre songs later made famous by singer Lotte Lenya. The evening itself was dedicated to Jean Genet, the ex-con whose explicitly homosexual and robustly transgressive writings were acclaimed by Sartre. Sandwiched between were a small handful of poems, including 'Oath', which included the breathtaking line, 'Jesus died for somebody's sins but not mine'. Her performance also included two songs dedicated to outlaws, 'The Ballad Of Jesse James' and 'The Ballad Of A Bad Boy', and an early version of the death letter, 'Fire Of Unknown Origin'. There was also space for a short burst of guitar noise, courtesy of a beaky, studious-looking hairy behind her.

Smith's guitarist that night was Lenny Kaye, another New Jersey émigré who gravitated to the big city to live the rock'n'roll fantasy. The pair met – where else? – in Village Oldies, a record shop that specialised in hard-to-find vinyl. Kaye had recently written a piece for *Jazz & Pop* magazine titled 'The Best of Acapella', an enthusiastic evocation of the golden age of doo-wop. Smith was so moved by the piece that she decided to call him up. Soon, the pair began to hang out at the shop on Saturday nights, where they would spin old 45s by long-forgotten vocal groups such as the Deauvilles and the Moonglows and dance the night away.

But the New Brunswick-born Kaye had an even greater musical passion. During the mid-sixties, America had witnessed an explosion of groups, bowl-headed beat enthusiasts who had taken their cue from the raw R&B sounds then coming out of Britain. Armed with a pile of records by the Kinks, the Rolling Stones and Them, a backline of Silvertone amps and guitars, bags of attitude, overactive hormones and the promise of girls and, perhaps, a gig at the local high school hop, these stepchildren of the Thames Delta sound rehearsed in garages, became cult heroes in their own backyard and, if they were lucky, got to make a record.

Kaye, himself a veteran of a handful of recordings as Link Cromwell (a nod to Link Wray, whose 1958 guitar instrumental, 'Rumble', was so ferocious that it merited a ban), adored the amateurish ambition of these small-town cult heroes. These groups played for their lives, not for some huge record corporation that did its best to tame them. And if that meant that their guitars buzzed with distortion, that their songs of fancies and frustrations got mangled in the mix, then no matter.

This subculture of so-called 'punk-rock' bands was the real thing, insisted Kaye and that small minority that was left asking what had happened to the true heartbeat of rock'n'roll. 'I think those were the best days ever,' wrote Lester Bangs in a highly influential piece, 'Psychotic Reactions & Carburetor Dung', published in *Creem* magazine in June 1971. He then corrected himself. 'I *know* they were.'

But those days were gone, swept away by giant waves of psychedelic improvisation and pastoral retreat. By the end of the decade, rock had been transformed into something deep, meaningful and grown-up. The 'goony fuzztone chatter' that Kaye and Bangs missed so much had been eclipsed by polite musical conversation, where expertise was everything and knuckle-chomping enthusiasm was uncool and infantile.

To virtually everyone else, who was more than happy to live in the present day, even the band names sounded positively prehistoric. Compared with the solid two- and three-syllable hard rock bands (Black Sabbath, Deep Purple, Humble Pie), the real-name sincerity of the singer-songwriters and the oh-

Beating the male rock rebel at his own game.

Smith, who recorded *Horses* at his Electric Lady Studio, always regarded Jimi Hendrix as rock's key visionary.

Two years before his death in 1969, Rolling Stone Brian Jones had predicted 'a new pop revolution'. Smith reignited the idea in 1975.

The alienated, teenage Smith took comfort in paintings such as Modigliani's *Draped Nude*. 'The women are built like I am,' she said.

It's a family affair: Smith in the 1970's with mother Beverly, and younger sister Kimberly, who sometimes roadied for her.

Total abandon: the up-and-coming rock 'n' roll poet poses for *SoHo Weekly News*, July 1974.

Preparing for *Horses*: producer John Cale issues instructions, Smith prepares to bark back. Visitor Mick Ronson and guest Tom Verlaine tune up.

Seeing Tom Verlaine's Television perform in April 1974 was the catalyst for Smith's reinvention of herself as a rock performer.

Smith's first friend in New York, Robert Mapplethorpe was also her flatmate, her mentor, her lover – and the man who shot the extraordinary *Horses* cover photo.

Like Smith, guitarist Lenny Kaye had an unerring belief in the power of rock 'n' roll to change lives. He compiled the influential 1972 garage-punk collection, *Nuggets*.

so-artfully named progressive acts (Yes, Genesis, Pink Floyd), definite-article-prefaced acts, such as *the* Standells, *the* Knickerbockers and *the* Count Five, sounded as authentic as that TV cartoon combo the Archies.

Lenny Kaye begged to differ. Like Lester Bangs, like Patti Smith, like Nick Kent and Charles Shaar Murray across the Atlantic, he had grown frustrated by the bloated self-importance of contemporary rock. Drawing on his vast knowledge of pop marginalia, he persuaded Elektra boss Jac Holtzman to give him the opportunity to anthologise this much-misunderstood era with a two-LP set titled *Nuggets*.

Subtitled, cleverly, 'Original Artyfacts from the First Psychedelic Era 1965–1968' (cleverly, because the word 'psychedelia' still had some residual cachet, at least among those who believed that pop still possessed the power to alter minds), *Nuggets* made only a minor dent in the consciousness when it was released in autumn 1972. But it was a milestone for its virtually inventing the idea of pop archaeology. Until then, trying to lay your hands on a record issued even one year before was almost impossible, unless of course there was a Village Oldies close at hand.

Kaye's accompanying sleeve notes, which documented what he called 'a changeling era which dashed by so fast that nobody knew much of what to make of it', made it clear that he regarded the collection as a mini-manifesto for change. Describing the 'berserk pleasure' contained within as evidence that 'something big was about to erupt', he lamented the fact that the late sixties flowering of rock had become 'hardened and formalised'. It was, he continued, 'a sure signal that perhaps it's time for the same old ritual to take place again'. And he didn't mean glam rock.

Both Patti Smith and Lenny Kaye sat back and waited. Once in a while, they cleared their throats in the pages of the music press, she spilling out stream-of-consciousness prose that probably owed as much to masturbatory fantasy as it did to conventional rock journalism, he littering his micro-histories of rock with chart placings and informed analysis.

In August 1972, well over a year after her debut as a rock'n'roll poet, Patti Smith was still preparing for change. Aside from returning to St Mark's Church for a Christmas Day 1971 poetry reading to prepublicise the (delayed) publication of *Seventh Heaven,* and a third appearance there during 1972, she had lain low. 'I started making my move when all the rock stars died,' she told Robb Baker a couple of years later. 'It just blew my mind, because I'm so hero-oriented. I felt total loss. And then I realised it was time for me.'

Smith had a slightly different explanation for Victor Bockris. 'I've spent half to three-quarters of my life sucking from other people,' she told him, 'and now I'd like to give some.' But, for the time being at least, she was torn between her role as a rock'n'roll domestic, caring for, and learning from, Allen Lanier, and her occasional sorties into the live poetry scene. She was not necessarily anxious about her twin roles. 'My pussy is being fed … so I'm not as fucked up as I could be,' she deadpanned.

'There's only one knowledge,' she insisted later, 'and that's the knowledge of what makes people come, what makes them go, Oh God! Like when you first heard the new Rolling Stones song, like when "Paperback Writer" first hit, or a Phil Spector song ...' Certainly, Grand Funk Railroad and Alice Cooper weren't doing it for her, and, across the Atlantic, Slade and T. Rex were no great shakes, either. For the time being, Patti Smith was content to remain on the rock'n'roll periphery.

But she wasn't entirely static. She wrote prolifically throughout 1972, while the following year saw the gap between her poetry and rock music begin to narrow. After a lengthy gestation period, Telegraph Books, co-run by Victor Bockris and Andrew Wylie, finally published *Seventh Heaven* in spring 1972. *Kodak*, a slimmer volume published by the Philadelphia-based Middle Earth, followed towards the end of the year. September 1973 saw the publication of *WĪTT* (pronounced 'white'), its 22 poems revealing a more abstract style with disjointed lines and a frisson of Rimbaud-style magic. For the frontispiece, Smith contributed a self-portrait line drawing of herself in glorious repose, naked and masturbating. A rhythm was generating.

As *WĪTT* reveals, the self-confessed 'iconographer' had now widened her circle of imaginary friends to include artist Georgia O'Keefe – famous for those shockingly vulva-like paintings – and Picasso, who had died earlier in the year. Of course Rimbaud was there too, 'sexy as hell' in the desire-filled 'Dream Of Rimbaud'. It's hardly a comfortable fantasy, which begins with Smith lying wounded, blood pouring from her eye. After taking a knife to his throat, she lies 'open as a cave', intoxicated by her 'total surrender'.

The poem that really outraged the feminists, though, was 'Rape'. As she reverts to her old habit of adopting the male role, 'Rape' follows the protagonist in lip-smacking pursuit of his 'lambie pie', whom he devours while jive talk rolls off his tongue. Once he's peeped 'in bo's bodice', and his victim dries away her tears, the pair get to their feet and jitterbug the night away. It was not an easy read, let alone when Smith – who liked to conceal her sizeable breasts by wearing a baggy white T-shirt – delivered it with manly conviction at her readings. It was a sure way to get noticed.

When Victor Bockris and Andrew Wylie brought Smith and Gerard Malanga over to London in summer 1972 to publicise a Telegraph Books anthology, she stole the show. Malanga had opened the event, reading, guru-style, cross-legged on the floor. Smith, sporting what Bockris calls 'her black Keith Richards hairdo', followed with a performance so dynamic that she even forgot the words to one of her new poems. (It began, 'The boy looked at Jesus as he came down the steps', a line eventually reworked into 'Land', the centrepiece of the *Horses* album.) After a moment's pause, Smith continued, improvising her way out of the impasse. 'The audience was completely blown away,' Bockris remembered. 'Nobody had ever seen anything like it.'

Smith was developing a style. She had, she admitted shortly afterwards, 'found a certain rhythm which is all mine'. She also began to think of herself more as 'a language architect' than a poet. Her lines had grown longer, her thoughts more fluid and abstract, her persona now a little closer to that of a sorceress. And, like Jagger, she had begun to learn how to work an audience. The whole point of performing, she said, was 'because you want people to fall in love with you'. She was trying harder now. 'I can seduce people,' she said, adding that she also had good punchlines, was dirty, funny and entertaining.

Smith had not just been watching Jagger. To find the true masters of the art of performance, you sometimes had to look beyond the world of rock'n'roll, she told Victor Bockris. Citing a compound of physical presence, intellect and a love for the audience, she invoked the examples of two contrasting characters, both of whom had used their powers for more dubious ends. Bible-bashing orator Billy Graham was, she conceded, 'a great performer, even though he is a hunk of shit'. Adolf Hitler, too. 'A black magician,' she insisted. 'And I learned from that. You can seduce people into mass consciousness.'

The way she projected was almost as important to Patti Smith as what she was saying. According to Penny Arcade in *Please Kill Me*, she 'lived her whole life pretending to be John Lennon or Paul McCartney or Brian Jones or some other rock star … She really had a romantic vision of herself.' It was true: she drew from gods, from monsters, but never from the mediocre. She looked like Keith Richards, smoked like Jeanne Moreau, walked like Bob Dylan and felt like Arthur Rimbaud. 'I was very image-oriented,' Smith admitted, wholly satisfied with her persona. 'All my toughness comes out of my desire to be cool and be accepted by cool people,' she added.

'Patti was so hot, so sharp,' reckoned Richard Meyers (later, Hell), a self-confessed 'hayseed' from Delaware who, like Smith, had worked in a store (Macy's) in order to fund his own Rimbaud obsession and poetic ambitions. 'But she was so sweet and vulnerable at the same time. She was the real thing, there was no mistaking it.'

By early 1973, when she would sometimes open for the New York Dolls at the Mercer Arts Center, Smith's poetry readings had begun to mutate into full-scale performances. She'd screw up her manuscripts and toss them to the floor, harangue audiences through a megaphone, accompany herself on a toy piano and sing and dance her way through her poems. It was as much an act as it was a reading, and people started to come to watch her perform, as much as listen to what she was saying. Contemporary poets such as Ann Waldman and Dick Higgins were literally left standing.

When the *Village Voice* caught her at Kenny's Castaways in May 1973, often regarded as the first Patti Smith 'gig', the paper described her as 'a cryptic androgynous Keith Richard look-alike poetess-appliqué'. She, in turn, started to call herself a comedian or a novelist. It was disingenuous, for, by that time, Patti Smith knew precisely where she was heading.

8. Rhythm and Alchemy

A bird flies from Patti's mouth. Television hit CBGB. Tom Verlaine's swan neck. The ghost of Jimi Hendrix. Patty Hearst and the new terrorist chic. Patti records her first rock record.

IN DECEMBER 1973, Patti Smith played a four-night residency at Max's. The headline act was Phil Ochs, a one-time potential rival to Dylan, though his refusal to turn his back on protest and embrace the new poetic surrealism consigned him to near obscurity. In retrospect, the billing appears an awkward mismatch, but at the time the pair – both committed to the people, the message and to hell with the fancy musical stuff – would have seemed reasonably well suited.

Eyewitnesses recall that Smith first appeared on stage with a pianist, though no one can recall his name. They ran through a few songs before she read some poetry. Then she brought on Lenny Kaye, the pair resuming their friendship the previous month after his lengthy sojourn in Europe. Plugging his guitar into his Princeton amp, Kaye accompanied Smith for a further three songs. It was nothing like their stage debut almost two years earlier. This was more like a rock'n'roll performance with poetry than a poetry reading with added rock'n'roll.

Serving to emphasise the change, Kaye played at maximum volume, often drowning out Smith's voice completely. But she barely noticed. Taking her cues from white jazz singers half-remembered from childhood, such as June Christy and Chris Conner, she experienced another one of her revelations during the short residency. 'It was like a bird flew out of my mouth or something,' she recalled two years later. 'I started singing ...'

She'd known it all along. 'Rock'n'roll was what I knew best,' she told Penny Green for *Interview* magazine earlier in the year. And, once she'd begun to make the transition, Smith realised that rock'n'roll came no less naturally to her than anything else. 'You don't know how much I struggle with every poem I do,' she said late in 1975. 'I struggle for hours, days, months. I don't know how to write it down. I don't know how to write a sentence or put it in tenses ... I can't make my poetry diamond hard like Rimbaud.'

Now her written work was genuinely blurring with rock'n'roll. During the residency, Smith had read the title poem from her 1973 volume, *WĪTT*. A five-stanza meditation on angels, cities, fools, and of course sex, 'Witt' is bleak, positing Smith as a survivalist in a twilit land of lost souls. Under the glare of Max's house lights, though, the piece lit up as Smith injected a new dynamic into it. 'I gave it a New York ballad rendition,' she told Tony Hiss and David McClelland for a major piece in the *New York Times Magazine* in December 1975. 'You know, let's keep on laughing, let's keep on dancing.'

Patti Smith had been twisting ever closer towards the rock market ever since teaming up with Jane Friedman, the veteran publicist who had booked her into the Mercer Arts Center and became her manager early in 1973. The 'Rock'n'Rimbaud' idea, which was how she'd been billed back at St Mark's in 1971, was revived for certain nights and it began to make much more sense.

After her period of exile, Smith was now willing to put herself about a bit. She sang the old standard, 'Baby's Insurance', at a Revillon-Saks fashion show, where she modelled Fernando Sanchez furs. 'He makes me feel like Anouk Aimée,' she told Penny Green, adding that, as well as devouring Dylan and Rimbaud, she'd also grown up reading *Vogue* and *Harper's Bazaar*. And, soon after hooking up with Lenny Kaye again, she asked him to join her for a reading at Les Jardins, a top-floor room at the Hotel Diplomat on Forty-third Street, where the pair duetted on the old Hank Ballard and the Midnighters' hit, 'Annie Had A Baby', and a version of Julie London's torch song, 'Cry Me A River'. By the time she'd been booked for the Max's residency, Smith was itching to take things further.

Back in 1971, she had encouraged Jim Carroll to front a rock'n'roll band, but showed little desire to do the same herself. By 1973, with rock'n'roll idealism at an all-time low, Smith was prepared at least to venture a little closer to the line. Her reluctance wasn't for lack of encouragement. Steve Paul, one-time owner of the sixties hangout the Scene and latterly manager of both Edgar and Johnny Winter, saw her as a ballsy, Joplin-style rock'n'roll chick who could be moulded into a kind of Streisand for the seventies. (He'd clearly identified a gap in the market, for another non-native New Yorker, Bette Midler, stepped in to fill that one.) He also suggested she work with Edgar Winter, then tried to put her together with whiz kid guitarist Rick Derringer, but Smith wasn't having any of it. She preferred the idea, once mooted during a long night at Max's, of an all-female trio featuring herself, Penny Arcade and ex-GTOs singer Miss Christine. Neither of her co-conspirators thought so highly of the plan the next morning.

Now, buoyed by her experiences at the Mercer Arts Center and Max's, Patti Smith was gaining in confidence. Early in 1974, she made another irregular live appearance, this time at Greenwich Village cabaret club, Reno Sweeney. Still awed by the experience some 18 months later, *Mademoiselle*'s Amy Gross recalled, 'This 27-year-old skinny punk who hammered out dirty poetry and sang surreal rock songs. Who never smiled. Who was tough, sullen, bad, didn't give a damn.' Smith was, she continued, a 'little Brando, a little *Blackboard Jungle*. A little Rimbaud, a little rapist, a little off the wall.'

That night, Smith came on like a ghostly apparition, her sunken face framed by a shaggy crow's nest of hair. Her clothes were jet black and seriously slimline, her fingernails bitten down to the skin. She read poems in praise of 'divine' vices, sang a song about cocaine, and another – the aching 'Break It Up' – about Jim Morrison. Other observers also recall a version of 'I Get A Kick Out Of You' dedicated to fellow Jersey kid Frank Sinatra ('The Picasso of America', she claimed), which she sang with a feather boa around her neck. That was a little uncharacteristic. 'She was a woman who dared to get up on stage and not aim to please,' Gross concluded. 'She was a dare: be bad, let it out, do it.' No one expected that from Maria Muldaur.

Smith was now seriously getting into role. The catalyst for her acceleration into the rock'n'roll clubs came on 14 April 1974, the night she and Lenny Kaye saw Television perform for the first time.

The pair had been to a screening of the new, ill-fated Stones concert film, *Ladies and Gentlemen … The Rolling Stones*, shot during their 1972 American tour, which had climaxed so spectacularly, at least Smith reckoned, at Madison Square Garden. Although a little of Jagger's alchemical performance was lost on celluloid, the film nevertheless confirmed their reputation as 'the Greatest Rock'n'Roll Band in the World', an epithet coined during their 1969 American tour that had stuck ever since. In truth, the spectacle of Jagger whipping the floor with his studded belt during 'Midnight Rambler' was more theatre than threat, but still the crowds roared him on.

The Stones had now been going for more than a decade; they had become an institution. Loyalty to the brand, the *idea* of rock as rebellion, was more an act of faith than anything else. The element of exotic surprise, which wild card Brian

Jones had provided so thrillingly back in the sixties, was gone. The Stones were still top-notch entertainment, no doubt about that, but their role in the forward march of the rock generation had come to a halt.

No one really expected to hear anything new, and certainly not anything extraordinary, from a rock'n'roll band by April 1974. And certainly not Patti Smith and Lenny Kaye, two of the rock underground's foremost chroniclers of an already bygone age. When they walked through the doors of the recently opened CBGB club, winding down after the movie, they were entirely unprepared for what was about to unfold on stage.

Like Smith and Kaye, Tom Miller had arrived in New York looking for music, culture and kindred spirits. Yet another avid bookworm, he'd landed a job at a second-hand bookstore called the Strand in summer 1968, and soon afterwards, struck up a friendship with Richard Meyers. They wrote poetry through the night, sharing an old typewriter, and, by 1971, Meyers was self-publishing magazines that featured articles on Arthur Rimbaud and Antonin Artaud, as well as his own work.

The pair also harboured musical ambitions, though it was only when they experienced the streetwise energy of the New York Dolls at the Mercer Arts Center that they felt confident enough to give it a try. Forming the Neon Boys in 1973, together with Billy Ficca on drums, the trio – Miller on guitar, Meyers on bass – recorded a six-song demo in a basement before a clash of personalities rudely curtailed their progress.

Miller, a classically trained pianist, had been the most musical Neon Boy. He was, after all, a fan of the Grateful Dead's superlative psychedelic epic, 'Dark Star'. So he decided to try it alone, with Meyers installed in the role of manager. The venture lasted no longer than an appearance on audition night at Reno Sweeney.

By this time, the pair were both working at a movie memorabilia emporium, Cinemabilia. It was when the store's manager Terry Ork introduced them to guitarist Richard Lloyd that Miller and Meyers reactivated the band idea. This time, it would be different. The guitarist grandly renamed himself after the French Symbolist poet (and lover of Rimbaud) Paul Verlaine – though years later he confessed that he'd not read his namesake's work at that point. Meyers adopted the decidedly less pretty name Hell. They rehearsed, mixing *Nuggets*-style covers, such as the Count Five's 'Psychotic Reaction' and the 13th Floor Elevators' 'Fire Engine', with a smattering of originals, and emerged in spring 1974 as Television. The name was unfashionably minimal, vaguely Warholesque, and entirely in keeping with the media-literate New York scene. The music, a blend of twin-guitar sophistication and rudimentary rock'n'roll moves, was not. It came from somewhere else entirely.

Patti Smith recognised Verlaine and Hell from the New York poetry scene, but she had no inkling of what to expect as they took to the CBGB stage. So rabid was her enthusiasm for what she witnessed that night that she broke with habit and wrote a piece on a contemporary band, published in *Rock*

Scene several weeks later. 'Boycott rock and roll on TV,' she declared. 'Who wants an image of the image?' Television had turned out to be the real thing.

With one short set, the group had completely restored her faith. 'Rock and roll is not Hollywood jive but the rhythm and alchemy of hand-to-hand combat,' she continued. Unlike the Stones, and all those big haired, blues-rocking behemoths that sought to break their box-office records, Television '... play real live. Dives, clubs anywhere at all,' she raved. Their music was 'pissed-off psychotic reaction', tunes to get knifed to, but no way was it cut from the New York Dolls' trash-rock template. 'They play like they're in space.' It had to be the work of seers, this roughly hewn transcendence masquerading as a rock'n'roll band.

The guitarist caught her eye too. Tom Verlaine's 'swanneck' was, she said, the most beautiful in rock'n'roll. His playing, tremolo-driven psychedelic bliss, yet needle-sharp, was no less unique. 'Like a thousand bluebirds screaming,' she swooned.

Having almost given up in her search for a new, young rock idol to worship, Patti Smith was hooked. Verlaine had a face like the artist Egon Schiele, a long, lean body not unlike her own, thought like a poet, played like a prince and possessed two of the most delicious necks in rock – one in his hands, the other on his shoulders. She'd fallen for him, and soon afterwards a relationship of sorts was being conducted surreptitiously over coffee, knishes and cigarettes at Yonah Schimmel's, a few blocks from CBGB.

Television's edgy, art-punk style didn't sound much like what she'd been doing in the clubs with Lenny Kaye and whichever pianist they could rustle up. But it didn't sound like anything else much, either, and that's what mattered most. It was rock'n'roll, though not as she or anyone else had heard it played. It made sense, and Smith was roused into action.

'When I first heard Tom play guitar, it was exactly like what I heard in my head,' she told Stephen Demorest. 'I realised it was what I'd been looking for. It was the same feeling I had when I was sculpting: it made me feel a quiet but noble power.' She even began to pick up a guitar. Unlike Verlaine, who had learned the basic rules before he decided to break them, she chose to ignore them altogether. She was already 28, after all, and in rock'n'roll terms time wasn't exactly on her side.

Inspired by what they saw, Smith and Kaye decided it was time to bring in a regular pianist. They tried out someone called Eric Lee, putting him through his paces on a sparse version of the old uptempo Wilson Pickett hit from 1966, 'Land of 1,000 Dances'. It didn't work out. Then Danny Fields mentioned that his current boyfriend, Richard Sohl, was a classically trained pianist who could play Mozart, the blues, virtually anything in fact.

Sohl knew it too, and Smith and Kaye took an instant dislike to the pianist's pompous airs. Sohl, who turned up for the audition dressed in a sailor's suit, gave the impression that he was auditioning them. When Smith discovered that the audacious young man with the thick mane of curly hair had been raised as a Jehovah's Witness, she changed her tune.

'We'd both rebelled against the same shit,' she recalled, 'and that helped. So we just brought him in.' Her only instruction to the new pianist was simple. 'What we want to do is go over the edge.'

Within two months of witnessing Television's call to arms, Smith, Kaye and Sohl were together in a studio, recording two songs intended for her first single. Not just any recording studio. The newly constituted trio were cooped up in Studio B at Electric Lady, the $1 million West Village sound factory built between 1969 and 1970 as a top-of-the-range workplace for Jimi Hendrix.

Smith had been there before, back in the days when she was on the outside looking in, at the studio's official opening on 26 August 1970. Inside, members of Fleetwood Mac, Johnny Winter, Yoko Ono and estranged Experience bass player Noel Redding were getting stoned and munching on Japanese food. Midway through the launch, Hendrix joined her on the steps outside. 'I said I was too shy to go in,' she told the *Observer*'s Simon Reynolds in 2005. 'He laughed and said, I'm shy, that's why I'm leaving. He told me all his plans, then he went to catch a plane to England for the Isle of Wight Festival. But he never came home.' Walking through the studio's hallowed doors in June 1974, she admitted to feeling 'a real sense of duty. I was very conscious that I was getting to do something that he didn't.'

The spectre of Jimi Hendrix hung heavy over the first half of the seventies. Endless cash-in compilations, as well as a deceptive repackaging of his pre-Experience recordings as a sideman, flooded the market. He was, as every musicians' poll allowed no one to forget, still the world's greatest guitarist. But, while his skills were keenly remembered, the idealism that fuelled his music had been all but forgotten.

Hendrix had ordered the construction of Electric Lady so that he could spend more time perfecting, and take greater control over, his work. He had been rock's most far-reaching visionary, the one whose music best embodied the counterculture dream of individual expression within a society that strove for harmony, progress and liberation. After all that had come to an abrupt halt on 18 September 1970, when he died, choking on his own vomit, Hendrix had quickly been reduced to a tragic virtuoso who, as Bowie eulogised on 'Ziggy Stardust', had simply 'played it too far'.

Despite her rock'n'roll-widow-like pilgrimages to the gravesides of her heroes, or her eulogies to Keith Richards, Marianne Faithfull and Anita Pallenberg, all of whom seemed to dice with death on a daily basis, Patti Smith did not believe that dying young was an inevitable consequence of the search for creative truth. Rimbaud had died young, so too had Jimi, Jones et al. She imagined what they might have done had they lived. She was going to survive.

As she walked through the doors of Electric Lady on 5 June 1974, Patti Smith – ever the necromancer – was determined to invoke the spirit of the dead guitarist. She had decided to record two songs, one an original, the other a cover. For the latter, she chose 'Hey Joe', the song that had launched Hendrix's career, and a Top 10 hit in Britain early in 1967. It was an inspired choice. 'Hey Joe' was a murder ballad, but in Smith's hands the tale of the man who shoots his adulterous partner gave her the chance to step inside a man's shoes, as she'd so often done in her poetry.

She also gave the song an added, hotly contemporary – and contentious – twist. Several months earlier, a little-known revolutionary group calling itself the Symbionese Liberation Army had shocked America with the kidnapping of the heiress and granddaughter of the late publishing magnate Randolph Hearst. Within weeks of her capture, 20-year-old Patty Hearst was caught on a security camera during a SLA raid on a bank. The grainy, slo-mo images began to tell a different story. Was this hollow-eyed, chalk-faced young woman with the long, feminist-cut hairstyle and a look of cool intent, a genuinely unwilling accomplice? The footage, not to mention the machine gun perched comfortably under her arm, indicated otherwise.

The suggestion that Hearst had made the transformation from super-rich respectability to manifesto-waving revolutionary mesmerised Smith. That she shared the same name as the most notorious woman in America was another omen. Not since Patti Page had there been such a famous namesake. (Patricia Nixon, daughter of the scandal-rocked president who rarely deigned to have her name abbreviated, didn't count.) Soon there would be two Pattis, both synonymous with controversy, both signifying danger to the status quo. Nomenclature – and who knows what else? – was on her side.

Smith prefaced 'Hey Joe' with a poem, 'Sixty Days', in which she explored Hearst's predicament. As they often did, her fantasies turned to sex. She speculated as to whether the all-American girl, 'standing there in front of the Symbionese Liberation Army flag with your legs spread', was 'gettin' it every night from a black revolutionary man and his woman'. As the poem segued into the song, the narrative of 'Hey Joe' was neatly inverted. Where the hell was Patty Hearst going with that gun in her hand? No one rightly knew, not even the shamanistic woman stretching her words, Dylan-like, into an Electric Lady microphone. But it made for a dramatic entrée into the world of recorded rock'n'roll, a venture that was sweetened by the addition of some delicious guitar lines from Tom Verlaine. The song ends with Hearst, like Joe, defiantly on the run and declaring that she was 'nobody's Patsy any more'.

While the single was marketed as a double-A side, it was the second track, 'Piss Factory', that received the lion's share of garlands. A surge of words, delivered with breathless abandon for a full five minutes, 'Piss Factory' recounted Smith's travails working at the Dennis Mitchell Toy Factory during that torturous summer vacation. Alienated and out of place alongside 'these bitches ... just too lame to understand', pissed off at the floor manager who told her, Dylan style, 'You ain't goin' nowhere', Smith recalls how James Brown singing 'I Lost Someone' on the radio and the smell of schoolboys with 'their dicks drooping' gave her comfort.

The fantasy of escape that brings the song to a climax rivals Bowie's *Ziggy Stardust* project in terms of vainglorious wish fulfilment. 'I'm going to get out of here. I'm getting on a bus. Go across the river. Go to New York City. Gonna be *so big*. Gonna be *so big*. Gonna be a *star*! *Watch* me now!'

The backing on 'Piss Factory' was minimal but dense, with Sohl's pace-setting, jazz-club piano dominating Lenny Kaye's minimal guitar frills. Smith also got her habit of quoting from other songs in early, with neat references to the old Isley Brothers hit, 'Twist And Shout', later popularised by the Beatles, James Brown's 'I Lost Someone' and Wilson Pickett's 'Mustang Sally' punctuating her monologue.

In the grand tradition of Simone de Beauvoir, Vera Brittan and Gertrude Stein, Patti Smith was utilising autobiography as raw material for her work. Now she too was poised to merge life dramatically with art, and find herself an international audience.

9. A Change Is Gonna Come

Patti impresses her peers. Finds a second guitarist. Visits California. Headlines CBGB with Television. Signs a record deal.

FIRST OF JANUARY, 1975. Patti Smith is one of 50 or more artists, writers and poets invited to perform at the St Mark's Poetry Project's New Year's Day Extravaganza. Several big names are there, including Yoko Ono, Allen Ginsberg and John Giorno. But it is Smith, with the now ever-present Lenny Kaye beside her on guitar, whose arrival on stage creates the biggest buzz. Hers is the voice of today and, so her peers nod sagely, quite likely tomorrow too.

As she introduces a new piece, a lengthy, trancelike synthesis of rock and poetry titled 'Land', Smith makes reference to the recently ended war in Vietnam. Violence, she says, 'the poetry of violence', is an American tradition that should not be forgotten. (Living in a city blighted by the social ramifications of metropolitan collapse, she would find that that wasn't too difficult.) 'But the thing about what's happening today,' she continues, 'is we don't put our violence in any man.' Violence is, she insists, 'a demon' that needs rechannelling, that requires transformation. 'And that's what art, that's what music, that's what rock'n'roll is all about.'

Two incidents that night serve as a measure of Patti Smith's transformation from rockin' poet to poetry-infused rock performer. Walking up to the podium, she passed Victor Bockris, her publisher at Telegraph Books. 'You owe me money, motherfucker!' Smith bawled, spitting on the ground before him. At the close of her set, with Lenny Kaye's incendiary guitar noise resounding around the room, she stepped off the stage, walked through the audience and right out through the door. Goodbye, genteel poetry gatherings; hello, rock-star postures.

Released the previous summer, the 'Piss Factory'/'Hey Joe' 45 was more a statement of intent than a planned attempt to launch a full-blooded recording career. Just 1,500 copies had been pressed in what was regarded at the time as a foolhardy – and largely unheard-of – music industry equivalent to vanity publishing. The disc did reach the ears of an executive at Atlantic Records, but there was little real hope that a record company would back a singing poet, especially one at such an early stage in her career. Besides, the notion of the limited-edition artefact had a long and fashionably cultish pedigree. Everyone from Rimbaud to Warhol via Crowley and Beckett had at some time, either for reasons of financial impoverishment or cult kudos, opted for the subterranean route into public consciousness. Both impoverished and mindful of the power of cult appeal, Smith relied on Robert Mapplethorpe, Lenny Kaye and Jane Friedman's Wartoke management company to put up the money.

The name she chose for the (largely notional) record label was revealing. Not without some deliberation, she settled on Mer, French for 'sea', thus revealing at once her Francophile tendencies as well as her affinity with one of the great symbols of art, literature and mythology. The sea, which represented both freedom and the feminine, would reappear frequently in her work.

The single, which was sold via mail order and in specialist record shops, largely relied on switched-on journalists and the rock'n'roll grapevine to spread the word. But it did its job in getting gigs for the 'group', as they now were, and it sealed Smith's switch from reading-room to rock-club circuit. Above all, it was tangible proof that she was, like Jagger, like Jimi and Jimbo, like Smokey and Dylan, a rock star of sorts. One small piece of plastic went a long way in the Smith firmament.

That summer, Patti Smith had transformed her fledgling trio into a fully functioning rock'n'roll band. They continued to work up her own writings into songs, and, to flesh out the set, she and Lenny Kaye raided pop's past for further material. This act, virtually heretical at the time, also served to align Smith with a particular strand of pop's glorious – and now largely forgotten – heritage. Given that Smith and Kaye both came of age at the height of the beat boom, it was little surprise that their version of 'Time Is On My Side' stuck closely to the

Stones' interpretation rather than attempting to ape Irma Thomas's gospel-inspired original. More pertinent still, they resurrected 'Gloria', the sexually charged, hard-bitten R&B hit for Them (featuring vocalist Van Morrison) in spring 1965. 'Gloria' was also a staple of the mid-sixties US garage-punk combos.

Both songs were carefully chosen, and then customised, to fit her needs. Smith, keenly aware that time was hardly on the side of a 28-year-old poet who'd just made her first record, prefaced the Stones' hit with a defiant 'Tick, tock, fuck the clock!' monologue. More artfully, 'Gloria' was topped and tailed with lines from 'Oath', Smith's poem from 1970. Instead of cranking in with one of the most illustrious three-chord tricks in rock, the song now began slowly, almost sacredly, before Smith waded in with the words, 'Jesus died for somebody's sins but not mine'. No one in rock had written a line like that in years – immediate, iconoclastic and truly breathtaking.

Facing a crowd alone intermittently for the past four years had served Smith well. She was now emerging as a natural-born entertainer, amusing audiences with lengthy monologues and nervously tugging at her *de rigueur* scruffy man's suit and white T-shirt. She also showed a keen awareness of the dynamics of rock'n'roll performance.

By the time she walked out onto the Max's Kansas City stage on 28 August 1974, for the first of a six-set, three-night double-header with Television, her set began with a blast through the Velvet Underground's 'We're Gonna Have a Real

Good Time Together', a regular opener in the Velvets' later live set. Smith had only recently come across the song while reviewing the posthumous *1969 The Velvet Underground Live* double set.

When she arrived on the West Coast for a short series of shows in November 1974, she'd added two further covers. The Marvelettes' 1967 hit 'The Hunter Gets Captured by the Game', written by her favourite Motown artist Smokey Robinson, remained in the set for the next year or more. Darlene Love's Spector-produced 'Today I Met the Boy I'm Going to Marry' didn't last much beyond the San Francisco show. The presence of such an eclectic range of cover versions in her set was way out of step with the times, but they gave Smith the opportunity to enthuse wildly about her heroes, and deliver lengthy raps on the 'true' meaning of rock'n'roll. There was an air of didacticism about these early Patti Smith performances, a blend of history and *her*story that was quite unlike anything seen before, and certainly not comparable to the rock'n'roll revivalist shows that had continued well into the decade.

The West Coast sojourn wasn't wholly successful: the shows at the Whisky A Go Go in Los Angeles (supporting British no-hopers Fancy) were poorly attended. But in San Francisco, where they ended up playing audition night at Bill Graham's Winterland venue, the trio experimented with a stand-in drummer – who many sources suggest was Jonathan Richman, something of a kindred spirit whose own Velvet Underground-fixated band, the Modern Lovers, had been struggling to find an outlet for their music since the start of the decade.

Going out on the road, albeit only for a two-city visit, had further whetted Smith's appetite. On her return to New York, she spent much of the winter incorporating more of her own material into the set, and – less gratifyingly – auditioning a revolving door of guitarists and bassists to flesh out the band's sound. The routine usually consisted of playing 'Gloria' or 'Land Of 1,000 Dances' for up to 40 minutes and hoping that one bemused hopeful might manage to last it out.

It was thanks to a bout of nerves that the terrier-like, Prague-born Ivan Kral just carried on playing. 'He ain't no genius, but he's got a lotta heart,' reckoned his new employer. Besides, Kral was 'so cute', and liked to play the part of a bona fide rock'n'roller.

The addition of a bass-playing guitarist fleshed out the sound, and Patti Smith chose to debut her new four-piece band closer to home, at the Main Point in Philadelphia. The main act that night was legendary British R&B shouter, Eric Burdon.

The real coming out of Patti Smith, however, happened in the spring, when, after first taking the stage there in February, she was booked to play CBGB for a night – and met with such a reaction that owner Hilly Crystal promptly booked her for a seven-week residency, playing four nights a week. And this time, at least at weekends, she was billed above Television thanks to some canny manoeuvres by Jane Friedman. That William Burroughs, Allen Ginsberg, Andy Warhol and their respective entourages dropped by on several occasions confirmed that Patti Smith had become the hottest, hippest ticket in town.

Initially known as a sleepy haven for the country, bluegrass and blues from which its now legendary initialism derived, CBGB had changed its music policy when Hilly Crystal saw his Sunday-night bar takings rise during Television's residency the previous spring. Now, with Max's temporarily closed (it reopened later in the year as Max's Kansas City), and the Mercer Arts Center defunct, the tiny Lower East Side club on the Bowery had become the focus for the New York underground scene, playing host to the Ramones and the pre-Blondie Stilettos, featuring Debbie Harry as one of three girl singers.

By spring 1975, both Television and Patti Smith were hitting their stride, and the love affair that had grown between Smith and Verlaine only served to heighten the creative sparks. With queues forming round the block each night, and new bands – Blondie, Talking Heads, the Shirts, Tuff Darts – forming virtually every week, New York was emerging as the most vibrant musical city in the world. The New York Dolls, who had planted the original regenerative virus, had just broken up. Now, a new wave of rock'n'roll evangelists were emerging to carry their cause into hitherto unknown spaces. When Television and Patti Smith presented a united front at CBGB that spring, it was, said Terry Ork, 'the official beginning of the scene'.

As the scene's most dynamic, articulate and mesmerising performer, Patti Smith was fast emerging as its figurehead.

On stage, she would beat her chest, simian style, along to the primitive rhythms cranked out by her band. She would ruffle her hair – now an unruly bob, like Louise Brooks in a sandstorm – and tug furiously at her Keith Richards T-shirt. Like an adoring fan finding herself face to face with the object of her desire for the first time, Smith just couldn't keep still or stop her nervous chatter. Most mid-seventies rock performers strutted around like prize peacocks or else feigned indifference. But Patti Smith could barely contain herself and wasn't afraid to show it. After all that devotion to the mad, bad and most dangerous minds in cultural history, it was as if she derived the most creative buzz of all from the audience.

In interviews, both vintage and more recent, Smith has often talked about 'putting rock'n'roll back in the hands of the people'. But it was clearly a two-way process, as she figured out as early as 1973, telling Penny Green that when she performs, 'I'm stealing from the crowd 'cause I need their energy, their need of me, their desire. Every time I see the Stones I feel as if someone has a rubber hose to my mouth and is drawing my breath out.'

Though Smith could still feel the magical relation between artist and performer on occasion (watching the Stones and Television, for example), much of that energy had been lost in recent years. Neither the stadium-packing power of Led Zeppelin and Pink Floyd nor the grand theatricality of Alice Cooper and David Bowie was capable of yielding the merest drop of sweat from the gawping crowd. The ritualistic elements of the rock'n'roll performance – hysteria, identification, total involvement – had been all but lost as bands became spectacles and fans spectators. There had been much hand wringing in the press concerning the growing detachment between the performer and the audience as the decade had progressed – which is probably why Charles Shaar Murray returned to London a changed man after his experiences in New York that spring.

As the most socially aware ex-Beatle, and the one who had clung most passionately to rock'n'roll as a life force, John Lennon had briefly attempted to reverse the trend. During nine days in 1972, he recorded a double album, *Some Time in New York City*, in a bid to realign the music with the people. Full of ballsy, highly politicised anthems, it misjudged the tenor of the times and met with a distinctly muted reaction. Piqued, he turned his back on rock'n'roll activism, split from his partner Yoko Ono, and headed off to the bars of Los Angeles, where he played out his mid-life crisis in the company of drinking buddies Harry Nilsson and Alice Cooper.

Lennon wasn't alone in rejecting the nirvana-seeking flamboyance of the late sixties. Everyone from Eric Clapton to the J Geils Band dressed down in a bid to wrest rock'n'roll away from the cape-wearing lords of prog, and the cheesy, diamanté flash of the glam rockers. But this bid to recast themselves as men of the people proved hideously counterproductive. It was an admission that rock music, once the symbol of wild youth, of wall-demolishing rebellion, was merely ordinary. It had slipped on a lumberjack shirt and a casual pair of denims, and pulled up a comfy seat with a pouffe on which to rest its tired legs.

In that slothful mode, it is little wonder that Bruce Springsteen – on his feet, a leather jacket slung casually across his back and peddling songs about cars, highways and eking out an existence in New Jersey – was heralded as some kind of saviour. He wrote taut, soulful songs about adolescence and working men, became a hero to a generation of cheese cloth-shirt-wearing rock fans crying out for some home-spun truths, and soon eclipsed all those other 'New Dylans' – John Prine, Kris Kristofferson, Loudon Wainwright III and even Cockney Rebel's Steve Harley in London – to become 'The New Dylan'. Dylan, too, was back. His 1974 album, *Blood on the Tracks*, which detailed his break-up with his wife Sara, was widely regarded as a masterpiece.

Both Dylan and 'The Boss' from Asbury Park were lauded for their songwriting abilities, and their willingness to speak 'the truth', whether from bitter personal experience or from social observation. But there was a rugged, inviolable maleness about them that seemed to deny many of the hopes and possibilities epitomised by the dandies of the previous decade. They were small men singing about small worlds. The place where music was able to alter minds, at least for a few hours, was now in the discothèque, where the uplifting productions of Gamble and Huff (the real sound of Philadelphia) got the world on its feet again. Dance music – or, more sniffily, 'disco' – threatened to fill the gap. Critics, quite rightly, began to write of the imminent death of rock.

There were the occasional rare voices of rebellion. Early in the decade, the reggae sounds coming out of Jamaica had been dubbed 'the new underground', though the Stones' Keith Richards and Eric Clapton were content to appropriate the rhythms and leave its rebel energies back in Kingston. The hearty embrace by the white-rock crowd – thanks in a large part to Patti Smith, and the London punk rock scene – was still many months away.

A grassroots pub-rock scene, centred on London and Essex, had begun to emerge in Britain since the early seventies, though much of this was simply reheated R&B, beery and sweaty but offering little more than a good night out. America had it much worse. The old guard of the late sixties rock revolution had dropped the rhetoric and instead taken up singing smoothly produced love songs (Jefferson Starship, Country Joe McDonald) or, in the case of the Grateful Dead, traded in their acid heads for some ill-fitting space-cowboy hats. Evidently, the drugs hadn't worked.

All this served as a depressing reminder that rock, once such a vibrant form that had captured the imagination of an entire generation, had become a flat, arid, artless, pointless terrain. Its brightest stars were now dead, bitterly cynical or living in the half-light of personal retreat. Rock's sole means of illumination was the vast panorama of lit matches that had become the unwholesome habit of America's stadium audiences. Someone, surely, had the presence of mind to blow all that out.

Enter Patti Smith. A seven-stone weakling, and five foot

five in her bare feet, she had everything that the Class of '75 so clearly lacked. By the spring, everyone from New York in-crowders to London-based rock journos and record company executives had started to take notice. Smith was now a bona fide rock performer at the helm of a four-piece band. Her set, a dramatic confusion of vintage material and her own impressionistic pieces, was as convincing as it was unprecedented.

More than that, Patti Smith had developed an engaging stage persona, both smitten fan and all-seeing saviour. She'd joke and giggle nervously, like a schoolgirl forced into the footlights for the very first time. Then she'd steady herself and dive deep into the fantasy, laying down lengthy raps about the sanctity of rock'n'roll before losing herself in the miasma of sound that swelled around her. It was a tightrope walk that had audiences hanging on her every word and gesture. Likeable, charismatic and seemingly never fully in control of her actions – her concerts were often disorganised and marked by lengthy between-song breaks – Patti Smith looked and sounded every inch the true figurehead for change.

'I desperately wanted a god, but I wasn't ever satisfied, so art replaced it, and rock'n'roll,' she told *Newsweek*'s Margo Jefferson later in the year. 'Kids are so hungry – I'm trying to put new thinking in people's minds.'

It wasn't only rapture-starved rock fans and would-be musicians who had flocked to CBGB during her residency there in March and April. Lou Reed, who had seen her perform at St Mark's in February 1971, was back. The ex-Velvet

Underground frontman had owed his early seventies renaissance to the patronage of David Bowie, and now it was his turn to play star maker. Reed had recently signed a deal with the industry heavyweight Clive Davis, who had previously headhunted Janis Joplin and Sly Stone, and brought both Paul Simon and Bruce Springsteen to Columbia. Davis, who, since September 1974, had been busy establishing his own label, Arista, was that rare thing in the upper echelons of the music industry: a businessman with a keen ear, who took a genuine, almost paternal interest in his artists.

Patti Smith had come to Davis's attention earlier in the year when a footnote in John Rockwell's arts column in the *New York Times* revealed that she had already been courted by RCA. An A&R man at the label, Stephen Holden, had installed her band in the company's studio on Sixth Avenue for a demo session. Neither party had felt inclined to move quickly on the outcome. Despite the fact that the emerging New York 'street rock' scene was now attracting bands from as far away as Boston and Philadelphia, the record industry had been sniffily dismissive of it, hoping that it might go away and leave everyone in peace.

After his spring visit to CBGB, where he was reportedly 'struck by her presence', Clive Davis wasted little time in signing Smith. Wooing her with a $750,000 advance, a seven-album deal and a promise to give her control over the way she was marketed – unusual, especially for a new artist – Davis made Patti Smith his first major new signing to the label. He was convinced that her music was fresh and valid, and impressed by her presence as a performer. He was also impressed by her attitude. 'I'm not getting any younger,' she told him. 'I have to be in a rush. I don't have the strength to take too long becoming a star.' Since he was eager for Arista to break a new star, this was exactly what Clive Davis wanted to hear. He was certain that the label had a major artist on its hands, and confident that the first Patti Smith record would be in the shops before the year was out.

10. The Soapbox

Patti pulls on a Cult Hero T-shirt. Declares that rock'n'roll demands to be saved. A typical Smith set *circa* mid-1975. A short conversation with Bob Dylan.

NINETEEN SEVENTY-FIVE: these were glory days for Patti Smith, perhaps the most glorious days she would ever know. She had a band, an audience, a record deal and the prospect of an international career. Having spent the past decade bathing in the reflected glory of her idols, she was now poised to make her private obsessions noisily public. She was not going to let the opportunity go to waste.

'I'm history-oriented and I want to be someone,' Smith admitted in an *NME* interview. Her ambition went way beyond collecting a few favourable concert and record reviews. 'The things I'm writing now are like my first baby projects at merging poetry with rock'n'roll,' she continued. It was 'the birth of something new'.

For the best part of the next two years, Patti Smith became a one-woman evangelist for the rebirth of rock'n'roll. No one, not Elvis, not the Beatles, not Dylan, not Hendrix, and certainly none of the artists who filled their vacuum in the early seventies spoke so passionately, or with such energetic and evangelical zeal, as Patti Smith did during those months.

The Who's Pete Townshend, often regarded as rock's most articulate spokesman, had continued to explore the power of pop through a series of sometimes bitter (*Who's Next*), twisted (*Tommy*) and occasionally affectionate (*Quadrophenia*) concept-record projects. But since he had once boldly claimed, 'Hope I die before I get old', his biggest struggle was wrestling with the idea of becoming a middle-aged rock star. Marc Bolan, who in 1971 made a dramatic transformation from underground cult hero to T Rex-fronting teen pop phenomenon, had also argued that three-chord rock'n'roll was a vital force in the liberation of lost souls. But, while like Smith he spouted poetry and muddied up the gender roles, his invective had been aimed towards a quite different market. When he flattered his audience with a song titled 'Children Of The Revolution', he literally did mean children.

Since she'd been thrust into the public eye, Patti Smith's atavistic desire to spread the word soon went into overdrive. Wearing a T-shirt with the words CULT HERO proudly emblazoned across her chest epitomised the strategy. Hadn't her breakthrough been, at least in part, a supreme act of wish fulfilment? Smith certainly thought so, and she was not about to rein in her fantasies now. 'I've had my whole life planned out since I was a little kid,' she told *Mademoiselle* magazine's Amy Gross that summer. 'I knew when I was going to wind up in a gutter and when I was going to be in Carnegie Hall.'

Each step on Smith's convoluted path to making a rock record had been accompanied by a hike in awareness of her own potential. It was true: she had talent, fortitude and, so it seemed, good fortune. Now that she was about to join her spiritual forebears, she was gripped by an unquenchable desire to spill her fanciful notions about rock'n'roll all over the stage.

No one conversed with an audience the way Patti Smith did at the outset of her rock'n'roll career. Often oblique, elliptical and dripping in rock'n'roll argot, her raps were like those of a babbling messiah. It was as if a light had been switched back on. All the residual dreams of rock'n'roll as a potent force had returned. She had never fully accepted they'd died along with Jimi Hendrix and all those other rock'n'roll corpses, even if everyone else had. Patti Smith, through an extraordinary and unprecedented act of necromancy, was intent on disinterring them.

One monologue, delivered that summer, was typical. Mirroring the oratory skills of some of the biggest, baddest men in history, she first identifies the problem, then looks at how it may be solved in micro fashion, before concluding with a flurry of sucker punches that amount to an entire redrawing of the rulebook.

'I think it's real important that people in rock'n'roll stay conspiratorial,' she began. 'The thing that really distresses me the most in rock'n'roll today is how businesswise and competitive it's got. Groups aren't helping each other. They fight against each other, they become competitive. The opening act and the headline act hate each other and they're always trying to subterfuge each other. I've been really shocked.'

But things were changing. 'There's a lot of good things happening. Allen Lanier of Blue Oyster Cult is producing a demo for Television. Clive Davis gave them a couple of days in the studio … Blue Oyster Cult lent me their crew, and their crew never heads off and to me that's a really wonderful thing because rock'n'roll is a fantastic conspiracy, our biggest political key, the thing that's gonna give us the most power.'

And are you ready? Because rock'n'roll is gonna save the world.

'[That] political people are getting rock'n'roll stars to play for them or try to help them, shows how powerful rock'n'roll's getting. It's gonna be the biggest art the world's ever seen. I bet Alexander the Great right now is wishing he had a Fender! It makes me feel that there's fantastic hope. Everybody says art's dead or sculpture's finished or painting's through. To me, rock'n'roll is in its pterodactyl state, and it's ours and it's just gonna keep going higher and higher. We've gotta wake up and realise again how much power we have. They fought for it in the fifties; people died for it.'

Smith's raps grew more intoxicating by the month. Words spilled from her elastic mouth like machine-gun fire, a rat-a-tat-tat that ricocheted around the New York clubs, spreading a new gospel among everyone who saw her. She was a peculiar kind of saviour, this poet turned rock shaman – sha-woman? – who ate her words like an overeager schoolgirl, whelped like an Indian brave and yet had the fireside charm of another old hero, television host Johnny Carson. She had a soapbox and, boy, was she going to use it.

On 28 May 1975, her soapbox got a little bigger. WBAI Radio, the station that had hooked her up with the sounds of the British beat boom a decade earlier, invited her to broadcast live from the station's New York studio. Bootlegged almost as soon as it was aired, her hour-long set captures much of the loose informality of Patti Smith's live set as she hovered on the cusp of greatness. 'Boy, is that a long pause on a radio!' she giggles at one point, acutely aware that right across the East Coast, from Times Square to the swamps of New Jersey, an audience far greater than the ones she was used to just might be tuned in – and that included her parents.

'Mum and Dad, I'm not on anything!' she quips midway through the set. It was no fib, either. She preferred, as the rock world was soon to discover in a blaze of headlines, to get 'High On Rebellion'. But, for unsuspecting audiences, her rambling monologues, interspersed by blasts of primitive rock'n'roll and sprawling, symbol-strewn sound paintings, gave the impression that hers was the voice of a madwoman, an inmate in a grim building on the far edge of town where only medics and ashen-faced relatives dared venture.

Though she looked, behaved and performed in the manner of a woman possessed, Patti Smith had sharpened up her act considerably since her ramshackle Rock'n'Rimbaud days. The recruitment of Richard Sohl had been crucial, bringing elegance and an informed musicality to a band that otherwise relied on Kaye's rudimentary skills, Ivan Kral's novitiate neck stroking and Smith's persona, often interpreted as that of an amateur. Everything, though, was orchestrated by Kaye and Smith's instinct. Between them, they had 40 years of popular music to draw upon – from the two-minute-plus abandon of first-generation rock'n'roll to the ambitious sound paintings of Coltrane and Hendrix. And it showed.

'1-2-3-4!'

Few mid-seventies performers – nay, *artistes* – dared reveal such a basic grasp of rock'n'roll timing by introducing a song like that. Synonymous with the fuzztone R&B of the sixties suburban garage-punk kids, it was an admission of creaky skills and one-flop-wonder amateurism. By transforming a badge of shame into a virtue, Patti Smith used the count like a battle cry, a battering ram to the soulless fortress of flowery technique and workaday sloth.

'One, two, three, four!' was the first thing anyone heard at this and most Patti Smith shows during 1975 and 1976. It was the cue for a high-energy take on 'We're Gonna Have a Real Good Time Together'. When Lou Reed had sung it, his downbeat Brooklyn drawl undermining the runaway rhythm, this obvious show opener sounded quaintly ironic. Smith's group played it hard and fast, transforming it into an unqualified statement of positive intent. That she usually garbled her scat vocal midway through the song didn't matter one jot.

A few years earlier, Country Joe McDonald used to begin his shows with an insistent ditty titled 'Entertainment Is My Business', but it was all about himself. Patti Smith's message was all-inclusive – '*Togethaahhrrr*!', she'd yell as the song wound down to its applause-seeking finale.

'We're Gonna Have A Real Good Time Together' plugged Smith directly into New York's outré rock tradition. It subverted it, too, avoiding the more obviously deviant 'I'm Waiting for the Man', which Bowie had covered to death a few years earlier. Before getting to the meat of the set, the band next chose to breach the grand rock/pop divide, so marked during the early and mid-seventies, with a muddied Motown take on 'The Hunter Gets Captured By The Game'. While the will was there, the artistry was not, and the song was most notable for its relevance to the Patty Hearst case than for any genuine musical effect.

Any lost momentum was immediately made up for when Richard Sohl started up the four-chord piano refrain that underpins 'Birdland'. Another expansive Smith epic, this song became the centrepiece of her set in the months before *Horses*, not least because 'Land', the first and finest piece of rock'n'roll storytelling in the Patti Smith canon, had been rested so that its impact on the finished record would be more keenly felt.

Though 'Birdland' was prefaced with a rap about Wilhelm Reich, the radical psychologist who wrote about sex, fascism and the function of the orgasm, and part inspiration for the song, the piece evoked be-bop, both in its title and in the way Smith riffed around a basic theme. As she recited her lengthy monologue about UFOs, funeral cars and being 'not human', over a backing that grew ever more intense, it was as if she were vocalising a particularly inspired Coltrane solo. Lenny Kaye's scratchy plectrum rubs against deadened guitar strings, like the sound of a thousand hungry seagulls, only heightened the sense of a band in free flight.

After her 'long pause on a radio', and a daft quip invoking an old Beatles song ('Everybody's got something to hide 'cept for me and my donkey'), a blues-rock guitar riff that wouldn't have been out of place at a Hot Tuna show introduced a new song, 'Space Monkey'. The hook may have been familiar, though Smith's delivery was not, as she mangled her words and whooped her way through the choruses. A spoken-word section evoking the old Phil Spector girl groups only confused matters more. The song climaxed with (presumably) Lenny Kaye mimicking what sounded like an orgasmic monkey.

'Snowball', little more than a riff in search of a song, passed by with small significance. Unsurprisingly, it was dropped from the set some time around October 1975. 'Distant Fingers', which, like 'Space Monkey', was another original held back from *Horses* and released on a later album, was far more promising. With Ivan Kral switching from bass to second guitar, it's likely that this was a recent addition to the set. That's surprising, because 'Distant Fingers' – a teenage love song to an imaginary Martian boyfriend in the absence of a real one – reveals a quite different direction from that suggested by the groundswell of 'street rock' then electrifying the New York underground.

Similarly tender in its subject matter was 'Break It Up', an exquisite song of surrender that Smith had co-written with Tom Verlaine. Perhaps that helps explain the song's more conventional shifts in dynamics as opposed to the instinctive sonic rises and falls characteristic of Smith and Kaye's work.

Smith's dramatic reworking of 'Gloria' provided the obvious showstopper. Customised with her new preface, Van Morrison's ode to sexual conquest is given a magnificent mauling every bit as shocking as it was subversive. As the guitars scrub their way to a furious climax, Smith drifts off on one of her stream-of-consciousness raps. Out spills a roll call of classic guitar brands, each one associated with the golden age of rock'n'roll, followed by the obligatory Rolling Stones name check. Then Smith hits the Now – on stage, in her stride, reaching for the stars. 'And they got together,' she rails, turning her monologue inwards. 'And they looked for a drummer ... And I know that you're out there ... And I'm waiting for you ... and we will go ... and the rest will follow.'

So spellbindingly different was the WBAI performance and other shows from around this time that most people seemed to forget that Patti Smith was still performing without a proper backbeat. That was what Smith's onstage prayer had been about. The answer, prompted in part by manager Jane Friedman, was drummer Jay Dee Daugherty, who'd been playing the circuit with Lance Loud and the

Mumps. Daugherty hungered for rock stardom, though not necessarily in the cool, seemingly indifferent way that Smith and Lenny Kaye desired it. His energy, enthusiasm and callow cuteness suited the group's requirements perfectly, though his youth meant that he required a little background knowledge in order at least to begin to understand where his new employer was coming from. When he joined the band, in June 1975, Smith and Kaye gave him 'a crash course in everything. We'd tell him about the Arabs and sixteenth-century Japan and flying saucers.' What they couldn't tell him he had to go and find out for himself. 'The poor kid had to carry all these books and records home every night,' Smith remembered.

Clive Davis had little interest in the drummer, or the rest of the group for that matter, when he finally secured Smith's signature right after the WBAI show. His vision was not unlike her own: that she was a unique artist in her own right, potentially iconic and eminently marketable with all the makings of a female Bob Dylan. Even the band/star relationship in many ways mirrored that of Dylan's with the Hawks (later the Band), with Lenny Kaye playing the Robbie Robertson role as her chief musical foil.

To emphasise the connection, Davis pulled a few strings and engineered a summit meeting of sorts, bringing the two together in the full glare of the cameras backstage after Smith's 26 June 1975 show at the Other End, a club on Bleecker Street in Dylan's old Greenwich Village stomping ground.

Aware that true greatness was watching her from a

dark spot by the bar towards the back of the club, Smith couldn't stop herself from throwing in a few knowing references 'to show I knew he was there'. ('You got a lotta nerve sayin' you won't be *my* parking meter' was one that was noted at the time.) These weren't lost on Dylan, either, not that he revealed as much when he showed up backstage after the concert.

'He didn't have nothing to say to me, I didn't have nothing to say to him,' she told Nick Tosches in a penetrating 1976 interview for *Penthouse* magazine. 'When he walked into the room he was just a guy, a really cool guy,' she added. 'He ceased being Bob Dylan to me.' Four years earlier, Smith had been able to sit in a room and feel superior to Rod Stewart and Eric Clapton. Now she was sharing space with the man she'd once admitted to British beat chronicler Barry Miles that she'd learned everything from, and the pair of them circled each other, 'like dogs in a pit', leaving most communication to what Smith called 'telepathy'.

They did, she remembered, have a brief conversation about Arthur Rimbaud. It went roughly like this.

Dylan: 'What do you read Rimbaud in?'

Smith: 'English.'

Dylan: 'I read him in French.'

It was, Smith admitted to Tosches, 'totally teenage nonsense'. But she put the absence of meaningful talk down to the fact that the pair were 'two very restless people, and that creates a lot of nervousness'. OK, she added, she was shy, and always was when she was 'around really cool guys until

I get to know them'. When she met Hendrix on the steps of Electric Lady, they'd discussed the weather. When she sat with Jim Morrison in New York, they ogled girls' legs and debated which one had the best butt.

The best thing about the encounter between the man with the short, Amish beard, the beaten-up leather jacket and the hooped shirt, and the wiry woman, her hair now bobbed into her 'Artaud/Baudelaire look', was, she later admitted, hearing Dylan utter her name. Despite her three-quarters-of-a-million-dollar contract, and the hype machine beginning to work its way into the mainstream press, Patti Smith was still, after all, a fan. And she rarely let her audiences forget it.

'[Dylan] not only encouraged me but assisted me,' she said between songs at a subsequent show. 'He helped me, inspired me, encouraged me most of all in the direction of my poetry and keeping the band together. He thought it was really wonderful that we should merge poetry in a rock'n'roll context – something that he's thought a lot about but he's done it in a different way, especially the improvisations. Whenever I get scared in the middle of improvisation, or lose my thread, I often remember how exciting he found it. And he said a real neat thing. He said, "You've got the eye of an eagle and you've gotta keep a hold of it." So whenever everything gets blurry I buzz over the arena and get my eagle eye back; I zero back in on the right word ... It was great fuel for me.'

The night that Dylan dropped by to suss out the competition, the Stones were back at Madison Square Garden. Though fiercely loyal to their torch-bearing legend, which

was why she wore her Keith Richards T-shirt at the Other End, Patti Smith no longer had anything to learn from them. Her band was now hitting its own stride.

'She's going to blow some minds,' insisted Paul Williams, in a piece flagged by a cover shot of Dylan and Smith at the Other End in the 3 July 1975 edition of *Soho News*. It was a poignant date in Smith's Diary of Remembrance – 3 July 1969: RIP, Brian Jones; 3 July 1971: RIP, Jim Morrison. But this time the omens were good.

As the stakes got higher, Smith seemed to ride the tide of acclaim with an affable, Carson-like professionalism. At the Other End, she wandered through the crowd, laughing with friends and shaking hands as if she were working an American primary election. With 'We're Gonna Have A Real Good Time Together' and 'Gloria' still bookending the shows, 'Piss Factory' had been reinstated, 'Break It Up' was given extra punch now that Jay Dee Daugherty was there to make every shift in dynamics count, and the Stones' presence in New York was celebrated with an encore of 'Time Is On My Side'.

Unlike 'Hey Joe', which was chosen because of Smith's desire to invoke the spirit of Jimi Hendrix and her interest in the Patty Hearst case, or 'We're Gonna Have A Real Good Time Together', which bound her to a particular and iconoclastic rock tradition, 'Time Is On My Side' was introduced into the set for purely vainglorious reasons. Never mind the associations with Baudelaire, forever preoccupied with the inescapable passing of time, it was, so she claimed, the song that turned the 18-year-old Smith on to the white-rock tradition. And now, with her 29th birthday just months away, she was aware that her time had arrived, time to make the record that would confirm what she, and those who had begun to hail her as a new rock'n'roll messiah, knew already. It was time for *Horses*.

Part 3. Horses, or A Season in Hell

I

UP TO THE point she began work on *Horses*, life for Patti Smith had often been waged as a battle – against childhood illness, against all manner of orthodoxies in the home, at school and at college, with herself as she gave up her baby for adoption, against the competitive creative egos she'd met in New York, and more recently against the broken idealism that prevailed in mid-seventies rock culture. But none of this fully prepared her for the torturous clash of egos from which she would emerge with the watershed rock album of the decade, a record that, over 30 years later, in parts sounds like a template for a new musical vision that has still yet to be truly explored.

Horses is by no means a perfect rock record. Not every song has been sculpted with the hand of pure genius. Nor was it in any way easy to make. At the first day's session, the producer put the band through their paces and told them that they sounded 'awful'. Smith, in turn, lunged at him, did her best to ignore his suggestions, and shed tears and nearly a stone during its making. He likened the experience to a boxing match and went half crazy during the sessions. She likened the experience to Rimbaud's *A Season in Hell.* It was tit-for-tat from start to finish. But from all the grief and the unremitting arguments emerged 40 minutes of music that prompted the most dramatic aesthetic *volte-face* experienced in rock for years. The boundaries were smashed, and contemporary culture never looked, sounded or felt quite the same again.

The sounds that spilled from the grooves of *Horses* were shocking enough. The sleeve only served to magnify the impact. But it was the meanings inscribed in the record as a whole that did the damage, heralding the end of one cultural era and the birth of another. The tranquillity had been shattered. *Horses* exposed a series of raw, binary oppositions – rock versus poetry, words versus music, male versus female, primitive versus cultured, low culture versus high art, old/new, modern/postmodern and monochrome/Technicolor being the most obvious. In so doing, it amplified tendencies that had lain dormant in rock for almost a decade.

These awkward conflicts – some reopened, others new to the discourse – were personified in the clash between artist and producer. Smith was relatively new to the recording process and preferred one-take spontaneity. Ex-Velvet John Cale preferred to take a more considered approach, constructing the record by building up layers of sound, perhaps even utilising strings and other musicians. Smith had the finished record in her head. Cale wanted to tear the songs apart and force the band to develop them further through improvisation.

When *Melody Maker*'s Steve Lake later bemoaned the record's production, Smith told him, 'Forget about Cale. He had nothing to do with anything. I mixed the record myself. Blame me for the way it sounds. The album was spewed from my womb. It's a naked record. We ignored all Cale's suggestions.'

That may have fitted Smith's auteur-like view of herself, but it simply wasn't true. It was John Cale who had forced the band to invest in new equipment at the outset of the sessions, he who decided to place Smith's vocals dead centre in the mix, which did so much to shape the overall sound of the album. He wrestled with Smith's poetic energy, reportedly to the detriment of his own mental health, so that he – and she – might locate the true soul of the record. When the moment was right, he double-tracked her vocals, and encouraged her to mix the results. The outcome was something that none of the participants, not even Patti Smith herself, has ever managed to surpass.

From the clash between Cale's maverick professionalism and Smith's gung-ho temperament emerged a new creative impulse. It wasn't hard rock or garage rock or even punk rock. It was art rock, but not as anyone – not even Velvet Underground aficionados – had ever known it.

On paper, at least, John Cale's pedigree was perfect. As a founder member of the Velvet Underground, he'd been at least partially responsible for the development of a counter-aesthetic that only now, in 1975, was beginning to gain credence as an alternative to rock's Beatles-prompted dive into neoclassicism.

But Cale, who'd studied composition at London's Goldsmith's College and worked under John Cage and LaMonte Young, had more serious music credentials than most of rock's hopeful Haydns put together. While they tended to look towards the lush, late-Romantic symphonies of the late nineteenth century, or even opera, his training was more firmly rooted in the twentieth century, where Schoenberg's 12-tone approach had prompted greater emphasis on atonality and, eventually, textures, silence and repetition. It was a far cry from the progressives' baroque'n'roll ambitions.

While Lou Reed had written most of the Velvet Underground material, it was Cale who stretched them to the limits until most ears could take no more. His bass playing, so low down and dirty that it was on virtual speaking terms with the Devil, could cure the most violent constipation. When he bowed his viola, which he made screech like a psychopath on a course of primal therapy, most listeners assumed their stylus had suffered irreparable damage.

Cale was a fearless musician, and an iron-willed personality who could handle anyone. In 1968, he produced Nico's *The Marble Index*, creating a Gothic masterpiece out of harmonium drones, howling viola and the singer's austere, prayerlike melodies. He was more than a match for the Stooges, unruly rabble-rousers from Detroit, producing their 1969 debut album. More recently, he'd worked with Jonathan Richman and the Modern Lovers, aspiring new-wave romance seekers. If anyone had the instinct to oversee the debut rock album by a performer intent on radical change, that person was John Cale.

But Cale's production prowess had always been a sideline to his own solo career, which had seen him return to his first instrument, the piano, creating a string of often ornate and elaborate albums that belied both his velveteen past and deviant production interests. He'd returned to a more robust sound with his most recent release, *Slow Dazzle*, which included a version of Presley's 'Heartbreak Hotel' that was positively suicidal. A confirmed maverick, and a man not inclined to swallow the opinions of others without good reason, he was always going to be a risky choice as producer.

As impressed by Cale's solo work as she was of his pedigree, Patti Smith remained undeterred. Her first choice of producer had actually been Tom Dowd, who'd recently put Rod Stewart on the American map for Atlantic Records, but label figurehead Ahmet Ertegun – who didn't get Smith at all – was having none of it.

At Smith's behest, Jane Friedman put the call in to London, where Cale was then living, and the prospective producer was roused from his sleep – it was four in the morning there – to discuss the project. 'This voice jumped down the phone at me,' he told Lucy O'Brien for the *Independent on Sunday* in 1996. 'It was as if the conversation couldn't be contained in a phone call, it had to be done face to face.'

Smith's instinct to look beyond the facts already told her that the omens were good. 'I thought he had the most beautiful voice, the most beautiful Welsh accent,' she told O'Brien 20 years later. Like his fellow countryman Dylan Thomas, when John Cale opened his mouth, poetry just seemed to flow.

Flying over to New York, Cale caught Smith in concert, and was knocked out by her energy and physical presence. He asked himself, 'How do I capture it on a record?' Like Lou Reed, like Iggy Pop, like Nico, Patti Smith was no wallflower, no run-of-the-mill rock'n'roller. Never one to dodge a difficult task, Cale accepted the challenge. 'It was,' Smith admitted to O'Brien, 'the start of an unfolding nightmare for him.'

* * *

By the time they walked through the doors of Electric Lady studios in August 1975, the band had been well primed for their task. There wasn't an excess of material to work from, especially as Smith and Kaye had decided to keep cover versions down to a minimum, but the band came reasonably prepared. At first, Cale was horrified, not at the material but at the state of the band's equipment. Even after his keenly attuned ears had judged that everything had been tuned up correctly, such was the poor quality of the guitars – they had warped necks and old tuning pegs – that he suggested a complete overhaul before the sessions could begin in earnest.

Cale analysed everything, prodding the band to justify their instrumental parts, and Smith and Kaye to reassess the overall arrangements. Conversations between Cale and Smith soon became an exercise in what the producer called 'shadowboxing'. At one point during the sessions, which lasted for just over a month, the exasperated producer asked Smith why she'd chosen him for the job. 'Because your records sound so good,' she replied. Cale called her 'a bloody fool', and said she ought to have hired his engineer.

'She struck me as someone with an incredibly volatile mouth who could handle any situation,' Cale told Lucy O'Brien. Except perhaps, he added, making the transformation from being the cult heroine of clubland to a professional recording artist. 'Working in the studio immediately throws you back on yourself,' he said. 'Her strength and instinct was already there. I was trying to provide a context for it.'

It was not easy for Smith – the poet who answered to no one and whose band answered only to her – who found it difficult to relinquish control. *Horses* was not just a record. It was the culmination of everything she'd been working towards for the past decade. 'I was very, very suspicious, very guarded and hard to work with,' she admitted to O'Brien, 'because I was so conscious of how I perceived rock'n'roll.' For rock'n'roll, read herself.

'On my record, I'm trying to reveal as much about myself as I can,' she admitted to *Crawdaddy*'s Susan Shapiro during the sessions. 'Sometimes I sing great, and sometimes I sacrifice great singing for very human moments. I have to let people know I am as weak as I am strong or I'm never gonna make it.'

Smith's attempts to show vulnerability in her work did not mean that she was happy to compromise in the studio. Though she later admitted that she 'didn't know anything' about recording, she was hypervigilant in her bid to avoid 'becoming overproduced, overmerchandised and too glamorous. I was trying to fight against all of that,' she told O'Brien.

Cale, who characterised the struggle for studio supremacy as 'an immutable force meeting an immovable object', was a hard man to budge. 'I made it difficult for him to do some of the things he had to do,' Smith recalled, and, in the months following the album's release, she resented him for not always letting her have her way. Twenty years down the line, she was at last able to portray him as her enabler rather than as her enemy.

'No one before or since has ever been as patient about [my ideas] as John,' she admitted. 'Instead of throwing his hands up or being pissed at me, John got even crazier and more obsessive ... One time we drove John so crazy that he was falling asleep at the control board and banging his head on it trying to stay awake.'

Smith's fear that Cale was secretly trying to make a Beach Boys record, rather than resurrect the spirit of the Velvet Underground, was understandable. As the first person to come along in years with a game plan to revive rock'n'roll's fatty, slow-pumping heart, the new messiah of New York was carrying a heavy burden. 'It's a real honour makin' a record,' she told Susan Shapiro. She meant it. Patti Smith needed rock'n'roll. Rock'n'roll needed Patti Smith. Everything else had been a rehearsal for this moment.

But Cale did understand, and years later Smith was gracious enough to recognise that fact. 'John did everything he could to fight our fight for us, even in his sleep,' she told

O'Brien. 'I didn't know how to sing, but the band's adolescent and honest flaws – I wouldn't say weaknesses – John always left them in. If he could subtly teach us to enhance what we were doing, he did that. He saw that we were improving and sometimes, maybe, we hit strange notes or hit a very explosive place, but he let us fly.

'I drove us all crazy but I think we can look at it and say, we did this body of work together, it's intact, there's no compromises in it.'

II

'Jesus died for somebody's sins ...
... but not mine.'

EVERY ROCK artist aspires to make an entrance that no one can ever forget. Very few succeed. Nineteen seventy-three happened to be a particularly good year for the Grand Arrival. Bryan Ferry managed it on 'Do The Strand', his 'There's a new sensation ...' at the top of Roxy Music's *For Your Pleasure* album coming on like a particularly startling Hitchcock moment. So too did Bolan, the two dirty sweet chords that announced the start of '20th Century Boy', a glorious riposte to his cock-rock-adoring critics.

Patti Smith's attention-grabbing entrée was set up by a brief piano phrase that wouldn't have been out of place in one of those God-fearing rock operas fashionable around the turn of the decade – 12 sanctified seconds that gave little hint of the slate-wiping impact her opening words would have.

Smith wasn't just reminding the world what Nietzsche

had told them a century earlier: that God was dead, and that responsibility rested only with the self. She was putting her own martyrs, those who'd died in the name of rock'n'roll, to rest. She, Patti Smith, the pariah from Pitman who once ponied alone to 'Bonie Maronie', had seized the podium and, like a turned-on Billy Graham, read out the First Amendment in the Constitution of a new rock'n'roll era.

Not everyone held these truths, outlined over the course of the next 40 minutes, to be self-evident. Even the apparent blasphemy of the opening line sounded distinctly odd and out of place at a time when the rock lyric had generally plummeted into drivel. The only sin Jagger or Robert Plant or Bad Company's Paul Rodgers roared on about was finding no easy starfucker to bed down with for the night.

It was probably rock'n'roll's most momentous entrance since Little Richard bawled 'Awopbopaloobopawop-bamboom' at the top of 'Tutti Frutti' back in 1956, but Smith's first line is – like Lennon's quip about the Beatles being bigger than Jesus – much misunderstood. Back in 1972, she'd admitted to Victor Bockris that, 'When I say that bad stuff about God or Christ, I don't mean that stuff. I don't know what I mean. It's just a new view, a new way to look at something … It gives people a chance to be blasphemous through me.'

Although she'd rejected organised religion as a young teenager, Smith's quest for spirituality, for a cause, for a saviour, had dominated much of her life. 'I wasn't saying that I didn't like Christ or didn't believe in him,' she told *Melody Maker*'s

Chris Brazier in March 1978. 'I wanted to take the responsibility for the things I do. I didn't want some mythical or ethical symbol taking the credit for what I do.'

The lines that opened *Horses* had been adapted from Smith's poem, 'Oath'. The song they segued into was older still. US critic Dave Marsh once described 'Gloria' as 'the best truly dirty record ever' – and he was merely talking about Van Morrison's original. By taking a song so saturated in the clammy sweat of male sexual desire, and making it her own, Smith posed an instant challenge to rock's ceaseless phallocentrcity. There is no man in Patti Smith's 'Gloria', just one woman expressing her lascivious desire for another. For 5 minutes and 55 seconds, a no-males exclusion zone had been erected around rock'n'roll. Janis Joplin, who'd neither looked nor behaved in accordance with the rules of the male fantasy, had never done that.

Choosing to cover a song so closely associated with the mid-sixties garage-punk bands – the three-chord trick that provided the song's motor was deliciously simple to recreate – left Smith open to accusations of lazy revivalism. Those who took their rock seriously tended to regard such inauthenticity as a serious crime, up there with 'sell-out' hit singles and appearances on prime-time television variety shows. But Smith didn't simply revive, or even reinterpret, the song. In the manner of Led Zeppelin taking a germ of an idea from Robert Johnson, hers was a song extension – except that she chose to forego the lengthy bowed-guitar solo and interminable tom-tom marathon.

Its title now modified to reflect the virtual rewrite, 'Gloria (In Excelsis Deo)' was a thrilling new-for-old moment in rock'n'roll, up there with Presley's baton-passing routine with the old hillbilly boys, and the Stones' trade-off with the bluesmen of Chicago's South Side. And, like both Elvis and Jagger, Smith possessed a voice that lifted the material out of the grave and into the future now.

The strutting, high-speed, twin-guitar backing was scandalous enough. But Smith's defiantly upfront New Jersey drawl, interspersed with the best hard-fuck yelps since Little Richard, and an ecstatic tic that sent her ululating into the upper registers at the end of every line, was a revelation. No woman had perfected the male rebel yell so convincingly, nor given it its own specifically female mannerisms.

The song gave her 'the opportunity to acknowledge and disclaim our musical and spiritual heritage', she wrote in *Patti Smith Complete 1975–2006*. It encapsulated everything she held sacred in art, 'the right to create, without apology, from a stance beyond gender or social definition'.

With Smith's repeated 'made her mine!' victory cries still ringing over the song's hackneyed coda, 'Gloria (In Excelsis Deo)' gives way to a dramatic – though not entirely surprising – change of pace, as the clipped rhythms of a reggae beat introduce 'Redondo Beach'. Though still months away from her headlong leap into Rastafarianism, Smith had been introduced to the music of rebel Jamaica by Lenny Kaye, who'd no doubt read about Keith Richards's enthusiasm for reggae a couple of years earlier.

Musically, 'Redondo Beach' was no great shakes, the rhythms only skimming the surface of the bass-heavy roots rebel style that was already tearing up the production rulebook. 'It's actually sort of a rewrite of "Endless Sleep",' Smith said at one concert, virtually acknowledging the song's white-bread interpretation. Lyrically, though, 'Redondo Beach' further develops the lesbian theme outlined in 'Gloria'. After a lovers' quarrel, a body is washed up on a stretch of beach in Los Angeles favoured by lesbians and gays. The suggestion is suicide, though Smith has since claimed that the song grew out of a poem written back in 1971 when her sister Linda walked out on her after a row while they roomed together at the Chelsea Hotel. It was an unlikely lyric for a reggae song, but, then, perhaps that was the point.

With the idea of pacing pre-eminent in the production of a seventies rock album, the primary purpose of 'Redondo Beach' was to set the scene for 'Birdland', the *pièce de résistance* on the record's first side. Clocking in at over nine minutes, this song – actually a dreamscape that owed less to pop or garage rock or reggae than it did the lengthy jazz club meditations of John Coltrane or Roland Kirk – was the first tangible evidence that Smith was truly extending the boundaries of poetry-infused rock. She aspired, she wrote later, to become 'a human saxophone'.

After Dylan's accident in 1966, the surrealistic patchwork of images and energetic wordplay that had reached its apotheosis on *Highway 61 Revisited* and *Blonde on Blonde*, had been reined in, replaced by a more plaintive style that sought deeper meaning through a mix of quasi-religious symbolism and simplistic truths. Dylan's music reflected that, the Hawks' potent electric backing replaced by his rediscovery of the country tradition, and, later, a more sober soft-rock sound.

But no one who'd even taken themselves at least half seriously had been immune to the Dylan effect. Jagger and Lennon fell over themselves attempting to emulate his lyric riddles. Right on cue, the mass production of LSD during 1966 and 1967 transformed a generation of songwriters into pop sages, able to see the greatest significance in shoes, rainbows, rabbits, even the whitest shade of pale. It inspired some truly fine psychedelic pop, but the novelty soon wore off, and by the end of the decade no one – except perhaps Marc Bolan and Melanie – was writing odes to starry beards and anthropomorphised beetles any more. Rejecting the cheerful infantilism of the hippie era, they instead sought to reveal themselves as fully formed adults, who sang simple songs about themselves, their spiritual paths or – duller still – the plain ol' good times. Any musician who described him- or herself as a poet who didn't answer to the name Leonard Cohen virtually guaranteed disappointment. Too many self-styled rock poets had nearly killed the phenomenon.

'Birdland' changed all that. A hallucinatory narrative that starts out like realist fiction ('His father died ... '), slides into a diarrhoeic flow of symbolism via a loose sci-fi plotline and fades away on a few bars of onomatopoeic gobbledegook, 'Birdland' was a revelation. The song grew out of a piece titled

'The Harbor Song', where Smith and pianist Richard Sohl sparred in an effort to recreate the effect of birds flying underwater.

The version that ended up on *Horses*, though, developed from a four-minute song triggered by Peter (son of radical psychoanalyst Wilhelm) Reich's *Book of Dreams*. Thanks to the ceaseless prompting of John Cale, and the ghostly presence of Jimi Hendrix, it became an expansive 'Peckinpah science-fiction nightmare'. While the process drained both producer and singer, it was, Smith told Simon Reynolds, 'my greatest experience, as performer, on *Horses*'. And, when the exertions of the song threatened to overwhelm her, she closed her eyes and visualised the late guitarist with her in the studio, goading and guiding her towards a satisfactory conclusion.

A career high and quite unlike anything else heard in rock before or since, 'Birdland' was always going to be a tough ride for Smith, even without John Cale breathing down her neck. The passage in Peter Reich's memoir that inspired the song dealt with a child coming to terms with the death of his father. 'He kept going out into the fields, hoping his father would pick him up in a spaceship or a UFO,' she told Susan Shapiro. 'He saw all these UFOs coming at him and inside one was his father, glowing and shining. Then the air force planes came and chased the UFOs away and he was left there crying: "No! Daddy! Come back!" It really moved me.'

Into the song's terrific, achingly beautiful narrative, Smith weaves an intermittent meditation on the nature of humanity. The 'You are not human' / 'I am not human' / 'We are not human' triptych was, Smith told Simon Reynolds, 'really talking about myself. From very early on in my childhood – four, five years old – I felt alien to the human race. I felt very comfortable with thinking I was from another planet, because I felt disconnected. I was very tall and skinny, and I didn't look like anybody else, I didn't even look like any member of my family.'

Emphasising the link between the alien theme and rock'n'roll's potential for otherworldliness, 'Birdland' draws to a close by invoking the strange, wordless vocals of doo-wop and the early girl groups. 'Sha da do wop, da shaman do way,' she repeats, shedding new light on the music of the immediate pre-Beatles era that had been virtually consigned to history after the mid-sixties beat boom.

While the song's title refers to the flock of blackbirds that young Reich mistook for UFOs, it also evokes the father of bebop, Charlie 'Bird' Parker, who lent his name to a jazz club in New York called Birdland. There were neat parallels between what Smith and her group were doing and the original beboppers, who delighted in their cultish love of the esoteric, their style-driven and attitude-laden culture of rebellion. Louis Armstrong had once described the movement as 'the end of jazz'. Smith, too, was bringing some kind of era to a close. And 'Birdland', performed by a five-piece with her voice playing the virtuoso part (thus matching the classic bebop set-up), sounded every bit like the piece of music that would hasten the change.

After the subtle, ever-shifting terrains of 'Birdland', 'Free

Money' brings Smith's boundless imagination back on firmer ground. The only Smith/Lenny Kaye co-write on the record, it features a three-chord rise and descent that was simple enough for the north-east British punk band Penetration to cover the song so effectively on their autumn 1978 album, *Moving Targets*. The closest thing on the record to punk rock as the world would soon come to understand it, 'Free Money' was built around what the band called 'a field', a chord progression that was played repeatedly until an arrangement emerged.

Lyrically, the song was by far the least sophisticated on the album. Smith was inspired not by the pictures she saw in her head but by her cash-strapped upbringing in New Jersey. 'It's really a song for my mom,' she told Simon Reynolds. 'She always dreamed about winning the lottery, make lists of things she would do with the money – a house by the sea for us kids, then all kinds of charitable things – but she never bought a lottery ticket!'

The second side begins with a song that skirted more closely to a pop sensibility than anything else on the record. 'Kimberly', an affectionate homage to Smith's youngest sister, is the third *Horses* cut to take its inspiration from family life and also the most poetic and revealing. 'Kimberly' posits Smith as mediator/protector: above her the falling sky, in her arms a newborn baby, the 12-year-old Smith feels, she croaks, 'like some misplaced Joan of Arc'.

The main thrust of the song was prompted by an incident that took place shortly after Kimberly's birth. Across the street from the family home, an abandoned barn had been struck by lightning. Picking up her infant sister, Smith ran outside to see the building engulfed in flames, its occupants – bats, owls and buzzards – screeching their way towards safety. She prays that 'something will make it go crack' – cracks in the sky are a well-known metaphor for madness – before, satisfied with the effect of her own peculiar energies, her sibling relationship can proceed with unequivocal love.

'Break It Up' was a more typical Smith homage. Co-written with Tom Verlaine, who contributed some devastating birdlike guitar lines on the track, the song had come to her in a dream about Jim Morrison. 'I took this car to a clearing and I stopped and got out of this car and there was this big marble slab,' she told the audience at the WBAI broadcast. 'There was this light pouring down on it, all the grass was like hair, and there was this guy on the slab. It was Jim Morrison. He was laying there and he was human but his wings were ... like Michelangelo wings. They were made of marble and he was like skin and trying to break out of these wings. I just stood there and kept saying, "Break it up, break it up, break it up." And he did and he flew away.'

Like Morrison in her dream, Smith too had been freed. The sound of 'Break It Up' echoes the mood of catharsis, its soft/hard dynamics not dissimilar to the Stones' 'Paint It Black', with added power ballad bombast. The influence of Television was obvious, too, but it is Smith's peerless rock-star performance, complete with audible chest beating throughout the second verse, that dominates the song.

'Break It Up' was tough and concise, confirming that Smith was eminently capable of delivering her own powerful brand of rock'n'roll. It would take something particularly exceptional to follow it. Enter 'Land', the record's undisputed masterpiece, and the song that proved beyond any doubt that she was not simply re-energising rock'n'roll: she was redefining it.

'Land' wasn't simply one- or even two-dimensional rock'n'roll: it was the culmination of everything Smith had been working towards. Over the course of an awe-inspiring 9 minutes and 25 seconds, the dividing line between rock and poetry was ruthlessly, and quite magnificently, erased. Her words pumped out the rhythms, the musicians played like poets and the two elements conspired to create something that went way beyond both disciplines. 'Land' was vast in the telling (it was 1,070 words long), loud and labyrinthine in its execution and breathtaking in its ambition. With due respect to Johnny Tillotson, this, at last, was true poetry in motion.

Smith started work on 'Land', one of her first attempts to fuse music and literature, in 1973. Its real origins, though, can be found in Memphis, Tennessee, in the late fifties. That was where Chuck Berry, the Poet Laureate of first-generation rock'n'roll, created 'Johnny'. Johnny was the archetypal teenager who, roused into action by the driving backbeat of the new music, picks up a guitar and imagines his name in lights. Immortalised on 'Johnny B Goode', Berry's 1958 R&B hit for Chess, 'Johnny' became synonymous with the guitar riff that kicked off the record – and launched a thousand careers, including, of course, that of the Rolling Stones. Berry revived his creation for 'Bye Bye Johnny', Joe Meek eulogised him on John Leyton's 1961 hit, 'Johnny Remember Me', Bob Dylan had him fooling around in the basement on 'Subterranean Homesick Blues', even Nik Cohn wrote about him in his 1967 pulp/pop fiction, *I Am Still the Greatest Says Johnny Angelo*. Johnny had made it into beat literature, too, as the main character in William Burroughs's *The Wild Boys*, which Smith cited as a key influence for the song. It didn't matter that Elvis had joined the US Army, or even that the Beatles had split. There was always Johnny. Johnny *was* rock'n'roll.

In resurrecting Johnny, Smith was effectively massaging the mythological heart of rock'n'roll back to life. But rock'n'roll had changed, and so had Johnny. No longer was he the guitar-toting freedom seeker of the fifties, or the mixed-up basement boy of the sixties. Smith's seventies Johnny was no teenage dreamer, nor a self-medicating bohemian. He was at the centre of a life-or-death struggle that neatly mirrored rock's own internal conflict. Wounded in a vicious encounter with a knife-wielding assailant – which may or may not have been himself, for Smith inserts a mirror into the *mise en scène* – Johnny rises again, Orpheus-like, carried by visions of horses into 'the sea of possibilities'. In this dreamlike scenario, it's not clear whether Johnny is in fact alive or, like Jimi Hendrix – who Smith also claims helped inspire the song – dead. But amid the violence, the revived dance crazes of her youth, the poetic allusions to sex, the sea and suicide, the overriding sensation – 'Oh, go, Johnny, go!' she urges midway through the piece – is that the pop Prometheus has once again been unbound.

Musically, 'Land' is similarly rich in rock referentials. Once again, Smith employs the technique of song extension, this time building the song around the 1966 Wilson Pickett hit, 'Land Of 1,000 Dances'. Once again, the spectre of 'Gloria' is brought into play, this time via the song's central three-chord motif. The effect, akin to that of a dosed-up garage-punk band drifting in and out of rock-group consciousness, reflects Smith's multitextured narrative perfectly.

For John Cale, the recording of 'Land' marked the moment when everything clicked. 'It was not clear what persona this record was going to have until I had her improvise against herself,' he recalled, referring to the heterophonic crescendo in the second half of the song. At least as important as what she said was how she said it. 'She had a Welsh Methodist idea of improvisation,' Cale added, 'in that it was like declamation. Lou [Reed] was kind of psychological, but a lot of Patti's impulses came from preaching.' If *Horses* was the holy book of the new aesthetic, then 'Land' was its Sermon on the Mount.

'Land' also confirmed, just as 'The End' had done for Jim Morrison back in 1967, Smith's status as a fully fledged Rimbaudian *voyant*. She knew it too, her repeated cry of 'Go, Rimbaud!' midway through the song lingering long after the song's tempest had stilled. The overwhelming sense of neatness and convention that had blighted rock since the turn of the decade had been trashed. A new, potentially mutinous, hybrid of poetry and rock had been achieved, and Smith knew it.

'There's no reason why the two have to be separated,' she told the *NME* around the time of the album's release. 'I think

I've proven it with what I do with "Land" ... It's totally impossible to distinguish what is poetry from the poetry in that and the rock'n'roll. They're so integrated ... '

Both Rimbaud and Hendrix (who makes a cameo at the track's conclusion as a man 'dreaming of a simple rock'n'roll song') had been in mind when Smith introduced an obscure concept all of her own midway through the song: 'Brainiac-amour'. It was, simply, her way of describing those nights she'd enjoyed having imaginary sex with her fallen idols. 'Nothing sick about it, ya know,' she told Amy Gross. 'Me and Rimbaud have made it a million times.'

It was Hendrix, whose presence Smith felt every time she entered Electric Lady for another long session, who provided the inspiration for the record's parting piece. Recorded, so Smith realised halfway through the session, on the fifth anniversary of the guitarist's death, 'Elegie' sounded more like a coda than a finale. A short, slow lament to rock's most painfully absent dream seeker, it seemed to hover above and beyond the rest of the record like an restless spirit, its portent-filled piano chords offset by washes of iridescent slide guitar, played by Allen Lanier, who co-wrote the song.

While 'Elegie' brings *Horses* to an eerie, otherworldly close, it also reopened the feeling of mistrust between artist and producer that had marked the early days of its making. Lanier, Cale told Lucy O'Brien, 'obviously thought that he was due a certain kind of treatment, and didn't feel I was granting him the space. It escalated and escalated until it got a little frightening.' The episode clearly left its mark, and for months afterwards Smith bad-mouthed Cale whenever the question of the record's production came up.

Talking to Scott Cohen in 1976, Smith paid Cale a double-edged compliment, calling him 'totally inspired and technically deficient' – just like her and her band. If she hadn't been so old – the record came out on 11 November 1975, just weeks before her 29th birthday – she said she would have titled it 'Young and Unskilled'. Within 18 months, *Horses* had incited a huge shift in the rock aesthetics, releasing an entire generation from the brush-denim complacency of post-hippie culture.

III

DEFIANCE. There was no other word for it. And, at least not since the mid-sixties, no other record sleeve like it.

The Rolling Stones had gazed out, impudent and nameless, from the British cover of their 1964 debut album. To the American market, they were billed as 'England's Newest Hitmakers', but their expressions – as the teenage Patti Smith was only too aware – suggested so much more. Two years later, Dylan had appeared fuzzy, tight-lipped and tilted on his side for the sleeve of *Blonde on Blonde*, the expression of self-contained indifference accentuated by the chequered scarf wrapped around his neck.

After the Beatles commissioned the pop artist Peter Blake to design the cover of *Sgt. Pepper* in 1967, the art of the record sleeve went into overdrive. The simplicity of the unadorned, personality-led cover was no longer enough, not when there was a huge palette of colour and visual tricks at the designer's disposal. The simple personality shot fell into disrepair, becoming the artless tool of the all-smiling pop say-nothing. The cover of *Horses* changed all that.

Patti Smith overslept the morning of the *Horses* photoshoot, but it didn't matter. The photographer she'd chosen was her old friend, Robert Mapplethorpe. Besides, she had no intention of wearing anything other than the outfit that had virtually become her uniform, whether she was on stage or out on the street. Simplicity was all.

When she arrived at Mapplethorpe's makeshift studio, in the apartment of Sam Wagstaff, it was still daylight. A triangle of light that backlit the plain white wall was fading, so Mapplethorpe worked fast, alone and with his characteristic mix of confidence and nervous energy. He'd known his subject for the best part of a decade, and had photographed her many times before. He knew what he wanted; she trusted him completely.

The bard wore black and white, her 'Baudelaire dress suit', as she called it. Perhaps just a little too much black, reckoned the photographer, who asked her to remove her jacket. She did, slinging it over her left shoulder just like Sinatra, bringing her right hand up to meet the left in some kind of awkward symmetry. Mapplethorpe now had the natural contrast he wanted, her crumpled white shirt giving off an uneven white that grew darker within its creases.

Smith stood up against the wall, now virtually grey thanks to the effect of Mapplethorpe's triangle of light. Fixing his camera with dead-eyed and unsmiling expression, her face half bathed in shadow and her head slightly tilted upwards, Smith struck the pose that divided the decade in two. Here was a woman dressed in man's clothing, a woman whose entire demeanour virtually refused the gender rulebook, a woman who was beating the male rock rebel at his own game.

Writing in *Patti Smith Complete 1975–2006*, Smith maintains that the cover of *Horses* 'captured some of the anthemic artlessness of our age'. Surely, she is being coy. The first shot in a new age of semiotic guerrilla warfare, it gave advance notice of seismic shifts in the new cultural order, from casual to committed, colour to monochrome, apathy to action.

Smith's intention was, she said later, to emulate Godard's wife and muse Anna Karina. The outcome was more *Masculin-Féminin*, ironically one of the few mid-sixties Godard movies that didn't feature the wide-eyed, black-bobbed Danish-born beauty. More closely resembling a hybrid of Bob Dylan and Keith Richards, hair visible on her top lip, she looked, wrote *NME*'s Julie Burchill in 1979, 'like the winner of the international Dyke You'd Most Like To Take Home contest'.

The photograph resonated with the noise of sexual deviance, a clear indictment of the so-called unisex explosion that had taken place between 1967 and 1973. By the mid-seventies, men still wore their hair long (albeit rather less appealingly than they had done in the late sixties), and women could pull on a pair of jeans without outraging anyone except their fathers. But with the decline of the sixties rock androgyne, epitomised by Mick Jagger as Turner in the blurred underworld chic of *Performance*, and the discredited sexual high jinx of the glam-rock heroes, even the male's right to embrace his femininity had been rudely curtailed. Where that left most women, billowing fragrantly in their flowing Laura Ashley dresses and cheesecloth blouses, was very soon all too evident. 'They said I had a sick attitude for a woman,' Smith complained of one magazine publisher at the time.

Smith's unflinching warrior stance was as much a threat to the status quo – and especially Status Quo and their fellow rock machos – as her music was. Servitude was simply not on the menu.

Women had not been entirely absent from the rock scene during the early seventies, though neither confrontation nor rebellion, let alone issues of sexual identity, was particularly high on their agendas. Those whose names tailed off with a 'y', 'i' or 'ie' (Carly Simon, Joni Mitchell, Melanie) tended to sing about deeply personal issues accompanied by piano or acoustic guitar. Some women fronted bands, Janis Joplin-style: Maggie Bell (Stone the Crows), Elkie Brooks (Vinegar Joe), Sonja Kristina (Curved Air). Every once in a while, an all-woman act would emerge, such as Birtha or Fanny. But, by the middle of the decade, more traditionally feminine singers, such as Linda Ronstadt and Maria Muldaur, had eclipsed them all. The brightest hopes were the Runaways, a group masterminded by the maverick LA producer/prankster Kim Fowley, who was in no doubt that sex was the band's most potent weapon. That small throng of feminists who, months earlier, had booed and hissed Beach Boy Mike Love as he sang 'California Girls' would not have been impressed.

Two years before Smith's emergence, another singer who'd been enticed to New York by the prospect of meeting Bob Dylan had been creating headlines. JUST A WORKING-CLASS GIRL

LIVING OUT HER FANTASIES ran one, kicking off a piece by Nick Kent in *NME*. She was Bette Midler, who, taking her inspiration from pre-rock'n'roll vocal groups such as the Andrews Sisters, then proved Steve Paul's assertion that the decade badly needed its own ballsier version of Barbra Streisand.

But Midler was pure showbiz, with a personality as big as her proudly displayed cleavage, and a fan base that leaned heavily on the gay clubs. Though Smith was a skilled entertainer, she baulked at schmaltz. Virtually the same off stage as she was on it, this particular working-class girl's fantasies were purely concerned with art, not artifice.

By adopting the guise of the male rock rebel, Patti Smith thrilled many and confused many more. Rendering most of her contemporaries redundant, she riled the male-dominated cognoscenti in a way that few had done before her. Just two – widely contrasting – women stand out as antecedents whose work went way beyond the unspoken thresholds of gender respectability.

One was Melanie. Ostensibly a peace-and-love troubadour forever embedded in the Woodstock mud, she howled like a banshee, delivering her songs of hurt and confusion with little regard for singer-songwriterly restraint. Reviewing her *Live at Carnegie Hall* album in 1973, Nick Kent, a rabid champion of the outré male rock rebel, catalogued what he called 'Melanie's horrendous excesses – a voice which grates more than chalk against a blackboard, spastic melodies and guitar playing ... I'd almost rather go through a series of complex electric shocks on my genitals than sit through this album again,' he protested.

But for all her ear-shattering, gut-wrenching vocal candour, Melanie was a woefully imperfect model for Smith. Her songs were, as often as not, twee celebrations of childhood and innocence. At heart, she was simply a hippie chick who let it all hang out.

Yoko Ono was quite different. An experimental artist since the late fifties, she'd been well schooled in the art of provocation long before she met, and later married, John Lennon. Her influence on the Beatle was profound – and often excruciatingly obvious to his public, who baulked at each successive stage of his radicalisation. The pair photographed themselves naked in the name of purity; made a series of records that included lengthy spells of silence, the sound of an unborn baby's heartbeat and newspaper stories about the pair's activities turned into repetitive chants; and stayed in bed for a week in the hope that world peace would soon follow.

That Ono was Japanese and significantly older than Lennon only made matters worse. The result was a hideous witch hunt in the press, a thinly veiled campaign of sexist and racist abuse that held her responsible for the break-up of the Beatles, for Lennon's brave, though sometimes misguided, dive into politics and – who knows? – the continuing decline of the British Empire.

Had the wider public been exposed to her music, things might have grown uglier still, for Ono's work was at least as far-reaching as her conceptual art pieces. Her first album,

Yoko Ono/Plastic Ono Band, released in December 1970, remains one of rock's best-kept secrets. Utilising her voice as an instrument (which Lennon mirrored on guitar with some of the finest performances of his career), she went where no other 'rock' vocalist dared go – emitting sounds, often wordless, that defied every convention. Unlike Melanie, Yoko Ono sang – though her detractors preferred to call it 'caterwauling' – to music that matched her vocal ambitions, whether employing violent, avant-rock repetition, or simply 'feeling the space'.

Ono broke through musical barriers in a way that no *male* rock performer had previously done. In privileging textures, trance and spatial elements, her work defied what was understood to be the natural order of rock music. It was created with an artist's sensibility, it was free, and it was female. Grossly misunderstood, too. By 1973, Ono had dropped the musical radicalism and had taken a different route, writing bitter feminist tracts such as 'Woman Is The Nigger Of The World' and 'What A Bastard The World Is', and couching them in a more conventional rock-band sound.

Like Ono, Smith's most enlightened, free and aesthetically challenging work was at the other end of the spectrum from the 'How big is my penis today?' clichés that prevailed during the early and mid-seventies. 'We're a feminine band,' she insisted to *NME*'s Paul Rambali. 'We'll go so far and peak and then we'll start again and peak, over and over. It's like the ocean. We leave ourselves wide open for failure, but we also leave ourselves open to achieving a moment more magical.'

It was an interesting assertion, not least because Smith

often denied her sexuality, preferring instead to regard herself as open to both her feminine and masculine instincts. It could be argued that this oceanic attitude enabled her to create a genuinely 'feminine' music – songs such as 'Birdland' and 'Land', that peak and subside repeatedly, like – on a good day – the female orgasm. Freed up from the jackhammer approach of the overtly masculine rock bands, these extended pieces certainly created the conditions to achieve moments 'more magical'.

While Smith was extending, perhaps undermining, the stiffly male rock practice to incorporate a more feminised approach, a handful of female literary theorists were developing the notion of a particularly 'feminine' style of writing. One, Hélène Cixous, argued in her essay, 'The Laugh of the Medusa', that women's 'language does not contain, it carries; it does not hold back, it makes possible'. She called this '*écriture féminine*', defining it as poetic, nonrealist, anti-logic and truth, undefined and rich in unsettled fixed meanings.

Despite its designation, *écriture féminine* wasn't necessarily gender-specific. Cixous also argued that male writers such as James Joyce, Jean Genet and Stéphane Mallarmé were able to engage in *écriture féminine* because their work ran counter to the phallocentric tradition. Above all, the practice was acclaimed as radical and potentially threatening to patriarchy and the social system that supported it. Julia Kristeva, a contemporary of Cixous's who specialised in the symbolist poetry that Smith had devoured since her teenage years, wrote a paper entitled 'La Révolution du Langage Poétique'. In it, she concluded that 'poetic language' is 'the place where the social code is destroyed and renewed'.

When distilled to their essences, these arguments fell dangerously close to reinforcing age-old ideas that women were the sensitive sex and overly concerned with anti-rational feelings and matters of the body. But the simultaneous emergence of a radical new line in feminist thinking and Patti Smith's *Horses* was comprehensive evidence of a new, femme-fronted leap into the creative unknown.

Smith, though, was a more complex and contradictory role model than that. As someone who sought to explore both the feminine and masculine impulse within, she often regarded herself simply as beyond gender. When she wrote about heroines, she did so from a male perspective. When she wrote about heroes, she did so from the point of view of a woman. When she dressed in male attire, she was appealing to both sexes, a turn-on for all just as Anouk Aimée, Anna Karina and Anita Pallenberg had been for her and her male friends.

'The masculinity in me gets inspired by female,' she told Penny Green in 1973. 'I fall in love with men and they take me over. I ain't no women's lib chick. I can't write about a man, because I'm under his thumb, but a woman I can be male with. I can use her as my muse. I use women.'

Though women inspired her, though she defiantly flouted all those male-given clichés about the role of women, Smith was certainly no card-carrying feminist. In a remarkable exchange with Nick Tosches for *Penthouse* in 1976, she asked him, 'Who the hell would ever want to stick his hand up the dress of somebody who goes around calling herself something like Ms?' Recalling her anger the first time she received a letter that addressed her as 'Dear Ms Smith' she continued, 'A word like Ms is really bullshit. Vowels are the most illuminated letters in the alphabet. Vowels are the colours and souls of poetry and speech. And these assholes take the only fuckin' vowel out of the word Miss. It sounds frigid.'

After rejecting the notion that photographs of 'naked broads' were exploitative ('I think bodies are great,' she declared), Smith returned to her pet subject, language. 'Every time I say the word pussy at a poetry reading, some idiot broad rises and has a fit. If I wanna say pussy, I'll say pussy. If I wanna say nigger, I'll say nigger. If somebody wants to call me a cracker bitch, that's cool. It's all part of being American. All these tight-assed movements are fucking up our slang.'

Smith was unable to empathise with the wider meaning of collective liberation because she'd spent so long fighting for and working on her own individuality. In the way that she'd cloak herself in male garments and give them new meanings, Smith preferred to take the so-called language of oppression and utilise it to her own ends. Intellectual debates concerning patriarchy and the true nature of ideology were for the lecture rooms. High on imagination, and the power of the individual to transform his or her own life, Patti Smith preferred to create and to act, rather than deliberate coldly on matters of cultural theory.

If, as some critics might suggest, she was acting from within a male romantic tradition, then she was doing much to extend it. When her heroes were male, they usually embodied some kind of altered state, whether simply sexual or in terms of creative-spiritual transcendence. Hendrix, Jagger, Jones, Jim Morrison, even Little Richard – each one was an artful dandy whose sexuality oozed gracefully beyond a pure and direct maleness. 'I am interested in the feminineness of men,' she once declared. That was hardly surprising.

Smith's attitude towards women was a complicated one. Sickened by her own femininity when she was young, she had been a self-confessed 'tomboy' who hated the crinoline-wearing, lipstick-smudged domestic goddesses of fifties America. 'I thought it was so dumb,' she told Lisa Robinson. 'I didn't want to be a girl because they wore Elvis charm bracelets and I couldn't get into that. I had a Davy Crockett outfit.' The women of her youth all looked 'like platinum bull-dykes', she once said.

Giving birth in 1967 forced her once again to confront her femininity. In a poem titled 'Female', written shortly afterwards, she wrote, 'Ever since I felt the need to choose / I'd choose male. I felt boy rythums [*sic*] when I / was in knee pants. So I stayed in pants.' She sobbed when she used the public ladies room, and blushed at her underwear. In fact, 'Every feminine gesture I affected from my mother humiliated me.'

Ordinary women, like ordinary men, were of little interest to her. She aspired to be like Jo in *Little Women*, like Modigliani's muse Jeanne Hébuterne, then later still, like the masochistic Stella Kowalski in Tennessee Williams's *A Streetcar*

Named Desire. 'I don't mind getting knocked around a little,' she claimed. She then retreated into her 'old man, old lady' relationship with Allen Lanier. Smith once advised Todd Rundgren's girlfriend Bebe Buell to pose for *Playboy*. 'I'd do it!' she told her, adding that the magazine was as American as Coca-Cola and Andy Warhol. She also fantasised about Joan of Arc and Patty Hearst being fucked by their captors.

The one time Smith slept with a woman, she 'thought it was a drag. She was too soft. I like hardness. I like to feel a male chest. I like muscle. I don't like all that soft breast.'

That didn't prevent other women from desiring her, or projecting their lesbian fantasies on her. 'The reason I came to see her,' wrote Julie Burchill in October 1976, after seeing her at London's Hammersmith Odeon, was

> because she physically turns me on like no one else. The lights go on and Patti bounces to the centre of the stage. Sex might once have been pretty but now it's something much more fine, vicious, deadly: Smith might be chicken-faced and pigeon-chested but she comes over like a chance encounter up a dark alley. She's so sexy she makes the Runaways look like Sisters of Mercy.

Some have insisted that Smith had a love/hate relationship with women, adoring the unattainable, and admonishing the rivals. 'I noticed that she was always uncomfortable around Debbie Harry-type girls,' Bebe Buell once said. Certainly, there was no love lost between Smith and Blondie when both were vying for prominence in the New York clubs. She was later accused of trying to poach both Fred Smith and drummer Clem Burke for her own band. Patti Smith was not about to join the New Wave sisterhood.

In many ways, her ambiguous sexuality was a camouflage. Like much early colonial writing, her style mimicked the (visual) language of the oppressor, suggesting that a schizophrenic identity lay at the core. Under the folds of cultural play, Smith was essentially heterosexual. But just as being adrift in the desert had stripped T.E. Lawrence (of Arabia) of his sexual identity, so art and music provided a realm into which Smith could launch herself and explore alternative ways of seeing and being.

She admitted as much in *WĪTT*, her 1973 volume of poetry, which begins with a 'Notice' in which she describes herself as being 'without mother, gender or country'.

'That's just an artist statement,' she explained to Amy Gross in 1975, continuing,

> You can't worry about gender when you're doing Art on its Highest Level. I mean, Rimbaud talked about the male and female within him, Artaud talked about it, every great artist does. I'm working on it in popular forms, but the rules in my heart are the rules of art which are almost no rules at all, except to aspire for greatness, aspire to heavenly heights and all that stuff.
>
> I'm just saying that androgyny isn't a concern of mine.

Critics talk about that kind of stuff. I'm a woman and I love men, but also I enjoy women. Female images excite me more than male images. In my poetry, I write about women because I'm a woman and artists are very narcissistic. People are narcissistic.

At the end of 1976, after a head-spinning 12 months that had transformed Patti Smith from queen of New York to fêted rock celebrity, she was on stage at the Bottom Line in New York, on the final night of a week-long stint. 'You all worry whether you're fifty per cent male or fifty per cent female,' she told the tightly packed crowd. 'What you should be is one hundred per cent what you are.'

Days later, in conversation with Caroline Coon, a rare sympathetic voice at the *Melody Maker*, she elaborated further. 'The Greek consciousness was bisexual. That doesn't mean they had to be fucking men or women, or be into any particular sex game. It just meant that both sides of their brains were working. And that's what makes a great conqueror.'

By that time, Patti Smith's clarion call had been widely heard and rock music was changing fast, faster than Smith or any of her early champions could have imagined a year earlier. The rock community was already becoming hopelessly divided and Smith, who aspired both to speak to the street and to make superlative art, found herself adrift in an aesthetic no-woman's land.

IV

DURING A BREAK in the *Horses* sessions, Smith talked about her hopes for the album. 'I would love to do a record that had just three minutes on it that inspired Smokey Robinson,' she told *Crawdaddy*'s Susan Shapiro. It was an affectionate, generous quip, though Smith hadn't come this far just to please one man, however vast his talent was. With the full might of the Arista publicity machine behind her, she knew that *Horses* was her first and probably last chance to stake her claim for rock'n'roll immortality. And, as her onstage monologues and many interviews over the previous 12 months had clearly indicated, Smith was aware that she was making a record that had the potential to leave a distinguishing mark on rock'n'roll, perhaps even change people's lives, just as Smokey and all the others had done for her.

Interviewing the singer for Sandy Robertson's *White Stuff* fanzine in 1978, Jane Suck asked, 'When you made *Horses*, were you aware of the bomb you had unleashed on the rock'n'roll world ... You know, the people who heard it and saw the Book of Revelation?'

'I don't think so,' Smith replied coyly. 'I was aware of my commitment, of what I was trying to do. I mean, I was filled with a certain fire and a certain desire to communicate, but it still hasn't really hit me about that record.'

It had. The knock-on effect of *Horses* was everywhere to be seen. But Smith preferred to see the record in terms of her own development – and was especially keen to move on to the next phase. '*Horses* for me was a culmination of one period of work that had started with Lenny, a culmination of four years of thought, processes of study, of performance, of failure, building and rebuilding. So when I did it I immediately shelved it. As soon as I was finished, it belonged to the people.'

The full consequence of that baton passing would take several months before it properly manifested itself. In the immediate wake of the record's release, in November 1975, Patti Smith and her band capitalised on the publicity it generated with a well-planned campaign that would first take her around America before hitting Europe, where it was always felt her work would be more sympathetically received. For a debut album of decidedly cult appeal, *Horses* – pressed at a local record plant in her home town – did remarkably well, shipping 80,000 copies in its first five weeks of release, just nudging the Top 50 in the States, and, perhaps surprisingly, just missing it in Britain. Within a year, sales would pass the 200,000 mark.

Between 26 and 28 December 1975, Smith played seven sets at the Bottom Line, New York's swishiest rock'n'roll niterie on West Fourth Street, just down the road from the gutted Mercer Arts Center. A luxury 450-seater venue that had opened its doors some two years earlier, it was a step up from CBGB and Max's. Though the set was similar to the one she'd been playing earlier in the year, kicking off with 'We're Gonna Have A Real Good Time Together' and encoring with 'Time Is On My Side', there were a few noticeable changes. 'Land' had been reinstated, and a fairly humdrum (and never-released) new song, 'My Mafia', had been added. Despite her Smokey Robinson fixation, 'The Hunter Gets Captured By The Game' was dropped in favour of a trio of covers that more keenly acknowledged Smith's affinity with the tougher end of the rock'n'roll spectrum.

The choice of 'Pale Blue Eyes', sometimes dedicated to Hank Williams, the country-singing casualty who, she reminded audiences, 'died in the back of a car on the way to a gig', reinforced links with the increasingly voguish Velvet Underground, and gave some breathing space to a set that now largely comprised uptempo material. Stitched onto its back end was a rousing chorus of 'Louie Louie', an unabashed nod to Lenny Kaye's *Nuggets* and garage punk. Most surprising was a finale of 'My Generation', a brave move on Smith's part, for few acts had dared take on Townshend's anthem of teen angst and haul it up for inspection by a new generation. Smith's adaptation – which included a rather clumsy, 'We don't need that fucking shit / Hope I die because of it' – really came alive in the New Year when she toured the States with John Cale as support. The song was Cale's cue to join the band on stage, strap on a bass and demolish the audience's ears – and occasionally the ceiling – with the most ferocious bottom end they'd experienced in their lives. (A version of 'My Generation', recorded in Cleveland, Ohio, on 21 January 1976, was subsequently released on 45 as the flipside to 'Gloria'.)

Smith often ended the song – and the night – with a coda inspired by her newfound sense of invincibility. 'I'm so young, so goddamn young!' she'd rant repeatedly. Growing in confidence and stature with every performance, her brilliant fusion of futures and pasts finding favour wherever she went, Smith seemed to possess the energy of a teenager. But, despite the fan-ish sporting of her favoured Keith Richards T-shirt, and the ceaseless invocation of rock's rebellious tradition, she was now a 29-year-old woman who had already grown fond of describing her audience as 'kids'.

* * *

The band's arrival in Britain in May for two nights at London's Roundhouse as part of an eight-city European tour had been hotly awaited. 'Cult queen for Britain' was how the British press flagged up the shows, prompting much excitement for those thrill-starved audiences to whom the word 'cult' was usually reserved for those who had slid into a mysterious, and quite possibly drug-ravaged invisibility – ice cool names such as Syd Barrett, Nico and Marianne Faithfull. But Patti Smith – 'She's strange, neurotic and possessed of a powerful unconventional sexuality' ran a tie-in Arista ad – was alive and well and on stage in Chalk Farm, north London, the spiritual home of the late sixties underground and a fitting venue for a contemporary cult heroine.

For their £1.80, the wildly expectant audience got a suitably cultish pre-show DJ who warmed up with a connoisseurs' tapestry of delights, including John Cale's 'Helen Of Troy', a live version of the Animals' 'Let It Rock' and, hot off the press, Jonathan Richman and the Modern Lovers' 'Road Runner'. The support act, the Stranglers, dressed in black and already veterans of the pub circuit, played a set that sounded like some weird hybrid of the Doors and a vintage R&B band from the Thames Delta. No one quite knew what to make of it. Then came Smith, a red scarf around her neck, an assortment of jewellery dangling over her T-shirt, which was emblazoned with the legend LOVE RASTAFARI AND LIVE.

Someone – it turned out to be Sandy Robertson – threw a copy of Colin Wilson's *The Outsider*, his influential 1956 study of alienated figures in literature, onto the stage. Smith dedicated 'Land' to the Yardbirds' vocalist Keith Relf. An icon of sorts to the US garage-punk bands, the Brian Jones lookalike had recently died after accidentally electrocuting himself while playing guitar at home. But he certainly wasn't 'the man who invented feedback', as Smith so enthusiastically claimed. It was one of *those* nights. For two nights only.

Back in London five months later, she recalled the Roundhouse shows as 'one of the happiest memories of my life'. The cognoscenti, though, were as divided as they had been over the album. ENERGY IS BACK IN FASHION is how *Sounds* trumpeted Giovanni Dadamo's ecstatic review. 'When I first sat down at my typewriter,' he concluded later that night, 'all I wanted to do was type "It was great" over and over again until I fell asleep. It was great.'

Over at *Melody Maker*, Michael Watts – the man who had elicited Bowie's infamous 'I'm gay!' quote – was less convinced. 'They achieved an inspired performance of Minimalist Art, where, of course, very little happens at all,' he sniffed. 'Patti Smith is for those who like the idea of rock'n'roll, rather than its perfect execution.'

Those who were unable to get tickets for the London show were compensated by a two-song live-in-the-studio session for BBC TV's *The Old Grey Whistle Test*. Earlier in the decade, the programme had provided a rare outlet for 'serious' music, offering rare opportunities to see up-and-coming acts such as David Bowie, Roxy Music and, much to the distaste of the laid-back bearded presenter 'Whispering' Bob Harris, the New York Dolls. By 1976, *Whistle Test* had become as sleepy as the acts it promoted. The arrival of Patti Smith and her band in the studio was a serious shock.

Hiding behind dark shades, and wielding an electric guitar, Smith tore up the show's dozy reputation with two incendiary performances. 'Land' started out with a virtual whisper, her New Jersey drawl croaking ever louder as the band gained its locomotive breath. Five intoxicating minutes later, the song faded on a Richard Sohl organ drone, segueing into a pathos-packed version of 'Hey Joe' that climaxed with Smith and Kaye indulging in a spot of rock-star guitar heroics.

Spring '75: 'She can generate more intensity with a single movement of one hand than most rock performers can produce in an entire set,' wrote Charles Shaar Murray.

With Dylan-like wit and intelligence, the dishevelled cool of Keith Richards and the stage presence of Jim Morrison, Smith shocked the mid-seventies into action.

Patti Smith, 1976: just some misplaced Joan of Arc …

The stripped-down, shirt-and-tie'd *Horses* look was maintained for much of 1976, spawning many imitators in London and New York.

'Pasolini lives and fuck fascists!'. In bringing art and politics to rock 'n' roll, Smith prepared the way for the punk-inspired, late-seventies cultural revolution.

'Fuck you, asshole!'. Smith's relationship with the British press nosedived after her sandwich-flinging episode in October 1976.

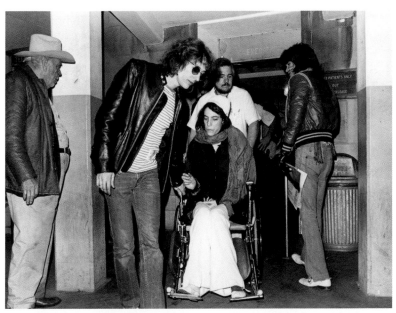

Smith leaves hospital after falling off the stage in Tampa, Florida, on 23 January 1977. 'I saw the angel of death,' she said later.

After her accident in 1977, the rock 'n' roll heretic underwent a personal renaissance, a search for what she called 'ecstatic religion'.

25 June 2005: Thirty years after its release, Smith performs *Horses* in its entirety for the first time at London's Meltdown Festival.

(Interestingly, Smith dropped the Patty Hearst introduction in favour of a pro-gay rap, 'If you are male / And choose other than female / You must take responsibility / For holding the key / To freedom.')

The May 1976 'British Invasion' had revealed both the best and the worst of Patti Smith and her band. The performances were fabulous, and rapturously received, as she reminded Simon Reynolds three decades later. 'I always think of us as a semi-English band because we were so maverick in America,' she told him. 'When we went to London and played that first date at the Roundhouse, the response gave me my first sense that, "Wow, we're really doing something".'

Yet, when a critic dared show up backstage afterwards to express some reservations, the mood soon changed, as *Melody Maker*'s Allan Jones discovered at some cost. Smith's mood of exhausted elation soon mutated into a look that was, he wrote, 'seriously deranged and reasonably fearsome'. Lenny Kaye became argumentative, swung a punch and ended up drenched in wine. Relations with the British press had got off to a poor start. Worse was to come.

* * *

Bad attitude, from the Velvets to the Dolls, had been a fundamental ingredient of the New York rock scene. A woman, a poet and above all a kind of fan-turned-singer who had somehow risen up from the streets, saviour-like, in order to rescue rock'n'roll, Patti Smith was giving it a new twist.

News that New York's antisocial rock elements might live in order to fight again had also filtered back to London via another route. Malcolm McLaren, proprietor of the Kings Road fetish clothing emporium Sex, had witnessed the winds of change during a spell in New York overseeing the final months of the Dolls' career. After arriving there in autumn 1974, he dressed the band in red patent-leather costumes, fashioned by his partner Vivienne Westwood, stuck them in front of a hammer-and-sickle backdrop and hoped that outrage would do the rest. But this was America. Even the bad boys and girls didn't touch communism – not even when it was played for laughs.

By the time he returned home to London, in May 1975, McLaren had already witnessed the wholesale eclipse of the New York Dolls by Patti Smith and Television. An acute observer of subcultural trends, especially those that chimed with his own belief in rock'n'roll as an essentially degenerate art, he knew that the city's underground was again on the move, with audiences lapping up bands that found themselves on the CBGB stage barely weeks after forming. The developing New York scene was tough, it was energetic and it carried more than a whiff of youthful rebellion. And McLaren had a hunch that London, then dominated by the self-congratulatory crowd that congregated at Tramp, badly needed something similar.

Since 1973, a growing pub-rock scene had emerged centring on bands such as Dr Feelgood, Eddie and the Hot Rods and the Kursaal Flyers. Preferring beer to bongs, worn leathers to fringed jackets and short, sharp R&B over lengthy solos and sweet vocal harmonies, the pub-rock bands were a reaction against the slothful, self-satisfied rock mainstream. They eschewed heroes, but there was not one genuine antihero among them. McLaren, whose shop traded under the slogan 'Clothing for Heroes', understood that every vibrant youth movement required faces to front it – from Elvis to the Stones, Hendrix to Bolan.

Arriving back in London, with New York Dolls' guitarist Sylvain Sylvain's white Les Paul under his arm for good luck, McLaren searched in vain for his antihero. His attempts to persuade Richard Hell, the lanky ex-Television bassist who'd already written his nihilistic anthem, 'Blank Generation', and with his torn, mutilated clothing, had patented the 'punk' look a good year before it exploded on the streets of London, had come to nothing. Hell was already embroiled in his next project, the Heartbreakers, formed from the ashes of the New York Dolls with Johnny Thunders on guitar and drummer Jerry Nolan. The group's first publicity slogan was 'Catch 'em while they're still alive'.

There was a self-destructive tendency in and around the New York underground scene that Patti Smith understood – after all, most of her heroes had died young – but had little interest in pursuing herself. Despite her pasty-faced image and uniform of poetic despair, art, music and stardom was for her a positive energy. She understood, as Rimbaud did, that in order to create it was first necessary to destroy. But while too many of her contemporaries would eventually be consumed by the first part of the Faustian bargain, she rarely lost sight of the dream that lay just beyond the danger threshold.

'I want to be successful,' Smith had admitted to *Crawdaddy*'s Susan Shapiro the previous December. 'Jesus wanted to be successful too ... He wanted everybody to see the light.' She was already preparing herself for sainthood, and the success of *Horses* and the euphoric receptions she received in Europe gave her further encouragement. Greatness, not an early grave, was what she craved. 'My creative instincts are with art, poetry and music,' she continued. 'I don't have any other motivation than to do something really great. I'd rather be a housewife, and a good housewife, admired by all the other housewives in the area, than be a mediocre rock singer. The only crime in art is to do lousy art.'

Until an untamed youth named John Lydon, from a rough corner of Islington, north London, walked into Sex one day late in August in 1975, the band McLaren had been working his Big Apple magic on had been little more than a younger, spikier version of the pub-rock bands. They played uptempo R&B and beat-group numbers from the mid-sixties, songs such as the Small Faces' 'Watcha Gonna Do About It?' and Dave Berry's 'Don't Give Me No Lip', while occasionally throwing in the odd Faces cover. Lydon, who was soon rechristened Rotten by his new band colleagues, had bad attitude. His wasn't an affected New York rock'n'roll sneer. It was *anti*-rock'n'roll, pretty much anti-everything. Not even his new playmates could fathom him. He mistrusted

McLaren, stayed at arm's length from the rest of the band, and stooped around threateningly like a sewer rat version of Richard III.

Better still, Rotten – another rock'n'roll Johnny – had a face, one of those once-in-a-generation mugs that can express the mood of the times and plenty more besides. McLaren instantly recognised it. He didn't care that Rotten couldn't sing, or that he had the stage presence of someone who clearly had no idea what he was doing up there. A homegrown Richard Hell who cared not a jot for art or ambition or anything else, Johnny Rotten was the perfectly imperfect face of the Blank Generation. But not just yet.

Patti Smith was well aware that some of America's most distinctive artists had to come to London in order to achieve recognition. Hendrix, she said, was a 'classic example', though she could have added Lou Reed, whose brief 1972 British tour and onstage appearance with David Bowie at London's Royal Festival Hall did much to seal the Velvet Underground's reputation, which had been growing in cult circles ever since.

But, the night after Smith's second Roundhouse show, a friend of Lenny Kaye's suggested they check out a new band down at the 100 Club in London's Oxford Street. It was the band McLaren had so desperately wanted ever since returning from New York a year earlier. It was the Sex Pistols.

'It was like, what a wacky name!' remembered drummer Jay Dee Daugherty. 'Let's go! So we get down there and it's like this dive – floors swimming in beer, and kind of grungy-looking people – not like punks, just sort of like ugly seventies people. This band comes on and we're like, whoa!'

Smith's thrill-seeking band members had barely had time to catch their breath before Rotten was haranguing them from the stage. 'Did anybody go to the Roundhouse the other night and see the hippie shaking the tambourines? Horses, horses, *horseshit*.' Daugherty's enthusiasm popped like a balloon. 'I said to myself, fuck, that was a quick fifteen minutes. We're over, we're fucking over already!'

'I was trying to do with the Sex Pistols what I had failed at with the New York Dolls,' McLaren said later. 'I was taking the nuances of Richard Hell, the faggy pop side of the New York Dolls, the politics of boredom and mashing it all together to make a statement, maybe the final statement I would ever make. And piss off this rock'n'roll scene ...'

In energising a generation of neophytes hip to a new aesthetic, and instilled with the belief that anything was possible, Patti Smith had created a Trojan Horse that carried within it the seed that would undermine her role as rock'n'roll saviour. According to her vision, art and rebellion would rush the rock stage as one. But, having built the portal through which London's peculiarly British take on punk marched, firing off shots in every direction (including hers), she found herself in a cultural vacuum, caught between the traditionalists and the great unwashed.

Unlike Rotten, Smith was a believer. She believed in rock'n'roll as art, as a force for liberation, in some ways as a healing process that would unite the world regardless of race,

gender or any other form of identity. The ideology of the Sex
Pistols was rooted in despair and negation. Belief was bogus,
art all the more so. They came, so the rhetoric powerfully
suggested, to destroy. But the effect of the Sex Pistols/McLaren
project was to reignite rock'n'roll in a way that even Smith
had not dared to imagine. For 30 years, Rotten has continued
to claim that this had nothing whatsoever to do with Patti
Smith and the 'Noo Yawk' scene.

'Everything that came out of [New York] was poetry-
based and too arty,' he once said. 'These people were much
older than us and had more old-fashioned attitudes.' Rotten's
disdain had already prompted him to write a classic putdown,
simply titled 'New York', which revealed his grasp for sarcasm
to the full. 'You think it's swell playing Max's Kans-ass,' he
sneered magnificently, before declaring that the city's 'bored'
and 'flash' musos were 'in a rut'.

Patti Smith's portmanteau of rebellion embraced both the
lofty aspirations of art, with its wild ventures into the realm
of metaphor and fantasy, and streetwise rock'n'roll. But the
Ramones, who flew in to play the Roundhouse a couple of
weeks after Smith's shows, had a more instant effect on
London's emerging punk scene.

While *Horses* drew much of its energy from the street, the
Ramones looked and sounded as if they lived on it, flick knives
and all. Young, dumb and with songs even Sid Vicious, the
Pistols' chain-wielding mascot, could hum, they had maleness
and an easy-to-replicate urban style on their side. Iconic in
their overgrown bowl haircuts, torn jeans and black leather

jackets, they were comic-book rock'n'roll rebels in a way that Smith, witch queen of New Jersey, was always too idiosyncratic and individual to be. Ramones songs were high on superfast energy, low on technique, were brain-pummelling, two-minute anthems, and their titles – 'Judy Is A Punk Rocker', 'I Wanna Sniff Some Glue', 'Beat On The Brat' – were as instantly memorable as their sound. The Beatles of the blank generation, the Ramones made Patti Smith and her group look as wayward, and sound as complex as Van Der Graaf Generator.

Part 4. After the Flood

15. 'Call Me Field Marshall!'

Patti flips her wig and starts hurling sandwiches. Punk in London. Radio Ethiopia. New York hots up. The Tower of Babel begins to topple.

OCTOBER 1976: Patti Smith was back in London, holding court in a reception room at the Intercontinental Hotel near Hyde Park Corner. She'd spent the summer in New York, recording the follow-up to *Horses*, and had just flown in after a series of dates on the Continent. Visibly tired, she'd turned up wearing an aviator helmet and shades, with the ever-present Lenny Kaye by her side for added protection. But if anyone needed sheltering that day, it was the press corps that had been rounded up to report on the woman fast becoming known as the High Priestess of Punk.

'Next question!' The usually loquacious Smith was in no mood for answering tricky questions that day. Especially unwelcome interrogations concerning her pulling power at the box office.

A rumour had gone round that tickets for Smith's two

shows at the Hammersmith Odeon had not been selling as quickly as one might have expected, given her cover-star profile over the previous 12 months. One brave soul decided to quiz Smith on the issue. It was the cue for one of the most infamous public tantrums thrown by a rock'n'roll star, and a key moment in Smith's self-induced defenestration in Britain.

'Fuck you, asshole!' she barked back. 'We can sell out anywhere!'

That was the cue for *Melody Maker*'s Allan Jones to enter the fray. Hardly endeared to the band after his experience backstage at the Roundhouse in May, he waded in with a few uncomplimentary words pertaining to Smith's guitar playing on the band's new record. Infuriated, she stood up, spat on the floor, sent ashtrays flying and then, picking up a plate of egg-and-cress sandwiches, hurled them in the direction of the journalist.

Neither the press conference nor Smith's relationship with the British press ever fully recovered from the incident.

In the light of the Sex Pistols' antics, which days later became a national story after a flurry of four-letters words on prime-time television, Smith's outburst was hardly more than a minor skirmish. But, while the Pistols had come across like a bunch of lewd comic-book rogues ('Fuckin' spent it, ain't we?', 'Wot a fuckin' rotter!'), Smith's bile-filled performance was regarded as silly, sanctimonious, defensive even, like an out-of-touch, old-school rock star.

Things had changed since her last visit. The Clash, one of a rash of bands formed in the wake of the Pistols, caught the mood of insurgency then sweeping the London clubs perfectly. 'No Elvis, Beatles or the Rolling Stones – in 1977!' was Joe Strummer's new and urgently barked battle cry of the neophytes. Unlike their New York contemporaries, motivated by a belief that they were saving their beloved 'rack'n'rawl', the new wave of British punk rockers showed no such respect. Patti Smith's loyalty to the Rolling Stones, who'd gone through the motions for six nostalgic nights at Earls Court in May that year, now sounded positively quaint.

'They still fill me with belief,' Smith railed at her increasingly mystified gathering, 'because the Rolling Stones, to me, have earned everything they have. For twelve years they've given us their health, their energy, their love, their devotion and their heart, y'know, an' if they're going in another direction I'll go right with them.'

After the episode of the flying sandwiches, the mood of the press conference went from crabby to surreal. Smith compared her brother Todd to Leonardo da Vinci, said she didn't 'give a shit' what Dylan was saying in his songs, described the title track from the new album, essentially a 10-minute guitar noise fest, as 'very sensitive, very heartful', and said she wanted Pierre Clementi, the Dionysian angel outsider of French new-wave cinema (and star of Buñuel's *Belle de Jour* and Pasolini's *Pigsty*), to play sax on her next record.

Smith hectored her audience on the responsibilities of a rock journalist, telling them, 'I was a rock writer once, and I wrote alone starving in my little room. It was such an honour to write about rock'n'roll ... ' She grumbled about life on the road: 'Like, I don't know if you guys are aware of this but, like, rock'n'roll is like really fucking hard work. It's, like, worse than being in the army.' A litany of complaints was not what the press had come to hear.

Smith left the podium with a rallying cry she'd repeat many times over the next two or three years: 'Call me Field Marshall! I'm the Field Marshall of Rock'n'Roll! I'm fucking declaring war! A war where everybody's fighting the same fucking war, man! My guitar is my machine gun!'

Her initial call to wage war against complacency in rock'n'roll was now being heeded, and with some genuine malevolence, but it was by no means the same struggle. *Horses* had brilliantly revived the tradition of three-minute rock'n'roll songs, but it was always much more than that. And there was her own acutely felt sense of personal mission, too, which, in this hour of mass revolutionary action, had left her quite alone.

'I'm not the kind of person who likes movements, dogmas, tests, rules,' she told Amy Gross back in 1975. 'I'm a real anti-person that way. Anything I ever got involved in, like religion, like school, these rules came down like a big shutter to shut out all the light from pouring in.' But, she added, 'I always admire change, and I see these movements initiating change.'

At the start of 1976, Smith told *Rolling Stone*'s Dave Marsh,

> I'm into rock'n'roll right now because there's a place for me. I don't think it's no accident that Bob Marley and me

should be coming up at the same time. Not because I have anything to do with Bob Marley – I just feel like a whole new thing's happening.

Rolling Stone in turn dubbed her, perhaps unhelpfully, the 'best new solo artist since Bruce Springsteen'.

Events in London had drawn her closer to her iconic, mass-market contemporaries, both of whom were, in widely differing ways, breathing new life into the rock mainstream. Like Marley and Springsteen, Smith was happy to stand above and beyond any mass movement and revel in her newfound guru status.

Arthur Rimbaud had rejected any suggestion that he was affiliated to any previous literary tradition. Jimi Hendrix spent the last months of his life trying desperately to extricate himself from the bondage of psychedelic superstardom. Patti Smith, too, was adamant she would not allow herself to be consumed by any wider movement. 'They're gonna have to change the rules, or maybe give the game another name,' ran the ads for the October 1976 shows at London's Hammersmith Odeon. Smith was in a genre of her own.

When she did acknowledge a bond with her fans, her errant offspring and her sympathetic contemporaries, it was usually explained in mystical terms. 'We are connected in some telepathic way,' she told Jane Suck in 1978, one of dozens of journalists to have transcribed the same rap. 'It's like that story that I keep talking about, the Tower of Babel story that I like, where God looks down and they're building the Tower. And he says, "Look at my people, they're as one ... So anything is possible to them." That's the key to the whole fuckin' thing, that if we do merge as one anything's possible.'

Caught in a double-edged war, in some part of her own making, between the traditionalists and the new rebels, and the bickering factions of punk in London and New York, Smith spent the summer of 1976 working on an album intended, so it seemed, to appeal to a wider audience. *Radio Ethiopia* was certainly more commercially oriented than *Horses*, with its polished HM rock production and use of traditional song structures. But, with a title track that occupied well over half of the album's second side, it also ventured deep into neo-psychedelic improvisation, prompting much debate in the process.

Unlike *Horses*, which was the culmination of four years' work, the bulk of *Radio Ethiopia* had been written during the band's first few months of success. Given that the title track was virtually a riff that soon dissolved into a freeform jam, and that two other songs, 'Ain't It Strange' and 'Distant Fingers', had been part of Smith's live set long before *Horses* had even been recorded, the record was something of a patchwork affair. But that wasn't to say that its intentions were unfocused.

Choosing to co-write four of the songs with Ivan Kral, the group member who most eagerly desired success, was indicative of a shift in Smith's priorities. Her musicians, too, were given a freer rein on song arrangements, so much so that when *Radio Ethiopia* reached the shops, in October 1976, it was credited to the Patti Smith Group.

The strongest signal that Smith intended to grow her audience came with the choice of producer: American hot shot Jack Douglas, who already had bestselling albums by Aerosmith and Alice Cooper behind him. Douglas's trick was to produce records slick enough to appeal to mainstream American tastes without sacrificing too much fire in the belly.

In commercial terms, the move clearly backfired. *Radio Ethiopia* failed to build on interest in Smith in Britain, while in the States it was virtually shunned, stalling at a miserable 122 in the *Billboard* chart. At a time when critics and fans alike rushed obsessively in an attempt to classify rock acts into Old Farts and New Wavers, it did little for her reputation either. Much of the table turning that had made *Horses* such a watershed record had been undone. Smith was unmasked as little more than yet another rock star willing to dilute her music in order to save her commercial skin. Worse still, she was seen to have failed.

But it was simply too much to expect that *Radio Ethiopia* would send shock waves through the rock community in the manner of its predecessor. Smith no longer held the wildcard of surprise, and, in any case, much had changed during the intervening 12 months. Yet those who turned a blind eye to the loud accusations of 'sell-out!', to the ritual chorus of platitudes concerning rock's proverbial 'difficult second album', were gifted with a record that was considerably more sophisticated than its predecessor, had been entirely self-penned by Smith in tandem with various combinations of the band, featured stronger individual songs with no concessions to pop ('Kimberly') or bleached-out reggae ('Redondo Beach'), and possessed much of Smith's characteristic linguistic richness. What it lacked was a 'Birdland' or a 'Land', authoritative confirmation that Smith had changed the rules and was sticking to them.

Instead, there was that notorious title track, 10 sprawling minutes on which the record's reception ultimately triumphed or foundered. Lacking both the elegance and the structural unity of its two lengthy antecedents on *Horses*, 'Radio Ethiopia' had more in common with the freeform improvisations of the psychedelic era. But there was a key difference between this and, say, Pink Floyd's 'Interstellar Overdrive', and that was Smith herself. She tore into the track with one of her so-called 'Babelogues', an improvised monologue that appeared to be a spoken-word equivalent to the 'automatic writing' favoured by the Surrealists. Pushing her delivery into a realm previously inhabited only by Yoko Ono, Smith never sounded more possessed on record, spewing out her words as if she were reinventing language from scratch.

'The closest to this voodoo and delirium that any male singer has gotten is [Tim Buckley's] *Starsailor*,' reckoned Simon Reynolds and Joy Press in *The Sex Revolts*, their 1995 study of gender, rebellion and rock'n'roll. They weren't far wrong. While stray phrases were vaguely discernible – 'Oh, you met your match in a bitch!' – Smith's voodoo vibe, recorded in one take on the evening of 9 August 1976, with a full moon in the sky, went way beyond the bounds of conventional rock, and deep into the realms of the unconscious.

Smith's uninhibited vocal was well matched by the band's performance. The track opened with 60 seconds of feedback-drenched sonic impressionism, which gave way to a fearsome, two-chord tribal thump – as if Led Zeppelin were covering Hawkwind – that played out relentlessly for the next four minutes. The remaining half of the song was an exercise in sonic disintegration, with Smith rambling incomprehensibly over a slow, drawn-out coda featuring a heavy dose of freeform guitar devilment. Once again, the spectre of Jimi Hendrix was invoked, via a steal from his Band of Gypsys anthem, 'Power of Soul' ('With the power of soul / Anything is possible'). It was the cue for Smith to fall down on her knees in Studio A at New York's Record Plant, and run her apprentice fingers up and down the neck of her newly procured 1957 Fender Duo-Sonic guitar while 'laughing hysterically, thankful for the privilege of playing in a rock'n'roll band'.

In many ways, *Radio Ethiopia*'s title track marked the apogee of Smith's desire to blast a hole in the complacent façade of contemporary rock and take it somewhere else entirely. But, to more cynical ears, it was too reminiscent of the stoned jamming of the late sixties' acid-rock bands, and quite out of step with the prevailing rush to bring excess to heel.

There was a suspicion of tokenism about this reckless finale of musical abandon, too, especially when the rest of the album had been so clearly tailored to more traditional tastes.

In pulling Smith's voice deeper into the mix, building layer upon layer of hard rock guitars, and beefing up the rhythm section, producer Jack Douglas had succeeded in refining the group's sound. With that in mind, 'Radio Ethiopia' sounded much like a guilt trip.

The album's opener, 'Ask The Angels', seemed to confirm the worst fears of those who had hailed *Horses* as a harbinger of a genuinely new approach to rock'n'roll. Hanging on a riff right out of the Keith Richards handbook, this was the Rolling Stones given a US-style makeover, loud and anthemic and packed with pomp-rock dynamics. The hook line, 'Rock'n'roll is what I'm born to be!', was hardly the 'wildcard up my sleeve' she claimed to have in her possession at the outset of 'Gloria' just an album ago.

As a curtain raiser, 'Ask The Angels' was as tame and predictable as 'Gloria' had been unexpected, and the immediate impression of an artist in retreat cast a heavy pall over the rest of the album. That was a pity, because, despite the clean-up act, Jack Douglas often managed to bring out the best in the material.

'Ain't It Strange', a spellbinding, mantra-like song that had featured in Smith's live set for well over a year, was dramatically transformed by the airy production. Though 'Poppies' took its musical cues from the clean, jazz-influenced backings utilised by the Doors on *An American Prayer*, it mined a rich seam of metaphor. 'Every woman is a vessel, is evasive, is aquatic,' Smith sang in barely a whisper, her voice once again pitted against itself as Cale had first done on 'Land'.

'Pissing In A River' closed the first side in air-punching fashion, and, though some of the guitar lines could easily have come from Jethro Tull's *Aqualung* album, the song was every bit the equal of 'Break It Up' in terms of passion and dynamics.

Though the album's second side was dominated by the title track, squeezed between that and the Stones-like 'Pumping' that opened the side was the delicious 'Distant Fingers'. A co-write with Allen Lanier, this yearning tale of extraterrestrial love found Smith hitting new levels of tenderness. One of her earliest compositions, it confirms that her work was never going to allow itself to be swallowed up by high-energy punk rock.

Radio Ethiopia contained songs of depth and quality. It also included an extensive prose piece – part autobiography, part art statement, part call to arms – written by Smith for the inner sleeve that wrestled with God, redemption and renewal just as her best poetry had done. Judy Linn's cover photograph, which once again set Smith against a bare white wall, eschewed the direct confrontation of Mapplethorpe's approach, and instead depicted her in artful, side-on repose. Looking intense and ravishingly beautiful, Smith could now rightly claim to resemble one of those French new wave cinema heroines she'd long aspired to be.

* * *

By the end of the year, Patti Smith was back in New York for the triumphant series of concerts at the Bottom Line. She returned to find the scene transformed. Many of her contemporaries had now been signed up, and CBGB, Max's Kansas City and the Bottom Line were now just the tip of a scene that had grown exponentially over the past year. Two compilations, *Live at CBGBs* and *Max's Kansas City 1976*, featured many of the newer arrivals, including the Shirts, the Laughing Dogs and (from Cleveland, Ohio) Pere Ubu, alongside veterans such as Suicide and the ubiquitous Wayne County. Neither set gave a particularly good account of the explosion of talent that had made New York the centre of the rock'n'roll universe for several months during 1975 and 1976.

Most of the significant acts had held out for their own deals. Smith already had two albums in the shops. The Ramones, snapped up by Seymour Stein at the newly energised Sire Records, had one with a second on the way. Richard Hell and the Voidoids, Talking Heads and the Tuff Darts were also on Stein's shopping list. Television had finally landed a deal with Elektra, with a debut album slated for February release. Blondie, fronted by Smith's nemesis Debbie Harry, had found a home for their reheated sixties girl-group sound with an independent, Private Stock.

One act had already grown tired of New York. Invited by Malcolm McLaren to join the Sex Pistols' Anarchy in the UK tour in December 1976, the Heartbreakers, fronted by ex-New York Dolls guitarist Johnny Thunders, had decided that London was about to become the centre of the rock'n'roll universe – and they were right. They flew into town just in time to discover that most of the tour dates had been cancelled in the wake of the Pistols' notorious appearance on the *Today* show.

The self-styled 'Field Commander Smith' was above these metropolitan scenes. BEWARE OF IMITATORS LISTEN TO THE ORIGINATORS! screamed the ads for *Radio Ethiopia.* 'Patti Smith has it in her to be to the seventies what Presley and the Stones were to previous decades,' declared a supporting quote culled from the pages of London's *Evening News*. 'She looks to be the first woman with style and energy enough to become a figurehead for a generation.' All that may have been true, but the Tower of Babel that Patti Smith built was already looking distinctly unsteady.

16. Fallen Angel

Patti falls off the stage and breaks her neck. Communes with God. Teams up with Springsteen. Scores a hit album and single. Introduces more vintage covers into her live set. Offends British journalists with her fourth album, and Italian fans by jamming with the Pope. Takes an honourable leave and gets married.

NINETEEN SEVENTY-SEVEN turned out to be the most crucial year in the cultural calendar for a decade. And Patti Smith, the liberator who had done so much to alter the sound and the style of contemporary rock 'n' roll, spent much of it laid up on her back.

The plan had been this. An extensive US stadium tour, supporting major mainstream guitar acts such as Bob Seger, Kiss and Ted Nugent, would capitalise on *Radio Ethiopia*'s rock-friendly production and deliver the Cult Queen to a wider audience. Then she would return to Europe in the summer, where she would be fêted as the First Lady of Punk Rock. But Patti Smith hadn't bargained for divine intervention.

On 23 January 1977, the band rolled into the Curtis Hixen Hall in Tampa, Florida, for the second date of the tour. A couple of songs into the set, Smith reached out for her microphone stand. She missed. Whirling like a dervish, she tripped over a monitor and fell backwards, 14 feet down into the orchestra pit below. Despite the best efforts of photographer Jim Marshall and her brother-turned-roadie Todd Smith, she hit the ground with a thud. Blood was spilled. Her band thought she was dead. In fact, she had broken several vertebrae in her neck and spine. Strapped onto a stretcher, Smith was hastily wheeled away and flown back to New York the next day.

To the salvation seeker, who had spent much of her life divining truths from seemingly cataclysmic events, her fall was interpreted as a clear message. 'Now all this sounds like mythical bull but it is truth,' she told *Melody Maker*'s Chris Brazier in 1978, continuing,

> Just like the guy at Altamont got shot during 'Under My Thumb', I fell just as I was saying 'Hand of God, I feel the finger'. And I did feel the finger push me right over ... I feel it was His way of saying, 'You keep battering against my door and I'm gonna open that door and you'll fall in.'

The song she'd been performing at the time of her 'swan dive' could hardly have been more appropriate. 'Ain't It Strange', a hymn to transcendence, had been in many ways Smith's challenge to God to make himself known. And now, she surmised, he had answered her call. That she had the fall was proof of the treacherous path she had been taking – and of her own inviolability. That she had survived it was an indication that she had friends in high places.

She told *Sounds* magazine by telephone a few days later,

> It was the most amazing thing that's happened to me. I'm like the kind of performer that courts risk. I court death. But the way I kept it together was totally relaxed. I saw, like, a spiral tunnel of light, and I felt my consciousness draining through it. I felt myself going and I said, 'Get back here!' I gripped my consciousness by the throat . . . the biggest battle was in my head, and I won.

Patti Smith had seen 'the angel of death' and lived to tell the tale. Like a 'Field Marshall, downed in the line of duty, I know I'll be standing soon,' she continued. 'Just tell the troops to keep fightin'.'

They certainly did, but it was no longer Patti Smith's benevolent cultural war that gave them reason to. Johnny Rotten, who had infamously appeared on the cover of a British rock magazine draped ironically and irreverently on a flower-festooned cross, signified something quite different from Smith's message of enlightenment through rebellion. There was no light, no saviour, simply the gleeful urge to destroy all that had come before him.

Smith's unfortunate accident prompted a quite different

emotion. 'After the fall, reconciliation is what we were about,' Lenny Kaye remembered. 'We got off the road. We had to cancel the European tour. We stayed home for a year, the year punk rock took over the world. We were there on the sidelines, really frustrated.'

Kaye had seen it all before. In a piece published by *Fusion* magazine in January 1970, he had surveyed the debris of the previous decade, and teased out some ground rules for the pop process. 'The way it works,' he wrote, 'is that someone picks up the torch and carries it for a while, and when they get tired, or irrelevant, or both, someone else does it for a time.'

Patti Smith was certainly tired, but, despite the mixed messages of *Radio Ethiopia*, she was hardly irrelevant. However, her fall did mark a key moment in her career, as drummer Jay Dee Daugherty has confirmed. 'Patti changed and came to grips with her own spirituality, and some sort of a spiritual system,' he said. 'She was working out some theme of resurrection and coming to a different place.'

That place, as was becoming increasingly obvious, was as far from the punk wars as you could get. 'Now, as for what I'm trying to do as an artist,' she said around the time of the release of her third album, 'well, the highest thing an artist goes for is communication with God.'

When Smith made her authoritative return – 'Out of traction, back in action!' – to rock's centre stage, in spring 1978, everything had changed. Television and Blondie were the darlings of New York, while in Britain she seemed a generation away from the one-chord wonders that had thrived during the so-called Summer of Hate.

'The whole great thing about rock'n'roll in the beginning is that it was offensive,' she told *Sounds*' Sandy Robertson, but that had little to do with the fists-and-spittle aggression of British punk. 'It offended because it had heart and adrenalin,' she continued. 'It wasn't a negative thing, it was a very positive, shining, physical burst of energy. It wasn't created to offend. It was created to spark, to inspire.'

Smith still talked up rock'n'roll whenever she could – 'My fight is to keep rock'n'roll alive and to continue rock'n'roll now more than ever,' she told *Zigzag*'s John Tobler in October 1977 – and she still had a thing or two to prove in terms of her own popularity. But her long lay-off, during which time she wrote a voluminous collection of poetry, prose and illustrations published in 1978 as *Babel*, had reacquainted her with the world of art beyond rock'n'roll.

'When I go into a museum and see *Bird in Space* or *Guernica* or Jackson Pollock's *Blue Poles*,' she told Robertson, 'I just feel so happy to be alive. I experience a certain ecstasy by greatness whether I do a good piece of work myself or someone else does it. My work isn't done but,' she added, correctly as it turned out, 'what I set out to do I feel that I've done.'

Smith had left Pitman, New Jersey, in the hope of finding herself an artist who would choose her as his muse. She exceeded even her own grand expectations by discovering the artist in herself, who in turn inspired a generation of others.

She had helped save rock'n'roll, but now she was almost entirely consumed by the act of saving herself.

Ironically, in turning inwards on herself, she emerged with what became the most successful record of her career. *Easter* was the moment of Patti Smith's resurrection in more ways than one. Commercially, it brought her the recognition she felt she deserved. Her highest-charting album on both sides of the Atlantic, *Easter* was also the first to spin out a hit single, 'Because the Night', which transformed her from cult status to a household name.

That was in a large part thanks to Bruce Springsteen, who was recording *Darkness on the Edge of Town* in the next studio at the Record Plant. The conduit was Jimmy Iovine, who'd engineered the blue-collar hero's *Born to Run*, and was now charged with securing a hit album for Smith. Springsteen provided a chorus that punched with all the bombast he was famous for, which Smith augmented with some of the most passionate, uncomplicated verses she would ever write.

This unlikely union of the New Jersey renegades further removed Smith from punk's centre of gravity. And, despite the glamorous rad-fem cover shot, with its defiant display of underarm hair, *Easter* was hardly going to impress the growing army of youths sporting Sid Vicious T-shirts. Once again, each side of the album began with an overly burnished trad-rock rallying cry, the opening 'Till Victory' easily eclipsed by the forced hero worship of 'Rock'n'Roll Nigger' in the rock posturing stakes. The latter's key hook, 'Outside of society / That's where I wanna be!', sounded as if it had come right off an Alice Cooper comeback record – and Smith's rock'n'roll growl only emphasised the point.

When held up against the shockingly original highs of *Horses*, these ventures into mainstream rock sounded clichéd, cartoon-like even. Arista's relentless hyping of Smith also started to ring hollow, especially in the post-punk era, when major labels – and their established stars – were viewed with mistrust. 'Poets are dangerous for their minds are free,' was the label's latest attempt to sell its greatest asset, though the fact that ads for the album were appearing in full colour in magazines such as *Cosmopolitan* tended to undermine any genuine sense of danger.

The record ended on a note of glory-filled self-aggrandisement, with Smith emerging from the prayerlike title track 'dying and drying as I rise tonight'. The belated inclusion of 'Privilege (Set Me Free)', augmented by Psalm 23, magnified the sense of martyrdom.

All this made the gaucheries of Smith's fighting talk more difficult to take. Continuing to insist that 'One of the reasons I started in rock'n'roll was to get rid of . . . the Doobie Brothers, Allman Brothers, that kind of laid-back American stuff' was one thing. But her high-speed warrior raps were rendered increasingly meaningless by repetition.

'I have American Indian in me,' she told *Zigzag* and virtually anyone else who came to interview her. 'I wake up every day and I'm half Apache. It's like I have nowhere to put my tomahawk so I have to scalp my electric guitar. My guitar is my instrument of battle. That's why I like rock'n'roll. It gives a little 100lb monkey a chance to be a soldier,' she insisted. 'My fight is to keep rock'n'roll alive and to continue rock'n'roll now more than ever.'

It sounded insincere. Dressed in *de rigueur* leather trousers and bowler hat, her eyes now circled by the thick black eyeliner favoured by the British punkettes, Patti Smith was no longer cheerleading from out front. She had other matters on her mind, a personal renaissance that, she insisted to *Zigzag*'s Kris Needs in 1979, had brought her full circle since the release of *Horses*, to an acceptance of a type of Christianity. 'I'm not talking about that Born Again jive,' she added. 'I'm talking about ecstatic religion. True religion as opposed to church religion.'

During 1978 and 1979, Smith's concerts grew closer to a travelling rock'n'roll nostalgia show, where covers of Presley's 'Jailhouse Rock', the Ronettes' 'Be My Baby', James Brown's 'It's a Man's Man's Man's World', Manfred Mann's '5-4-3-2-1', Dylan's 'Mr Tambourine Man' and the Byrds' 'So You Want To Be A Rock'n'Roll Star' started to sound like laziness rather than mining a hitherto undervalued rock'n'roll tradition. 'Radio Ethiopia' was conspicuous by its absence. She achieved her dream of supporting the Rolling Stones, declared that she simply wanted 'to have fun' and brought along an American flag as a backdrop for her European shows.

Her fourth and – for the time being anyway – final album, 1979's *Wave*, confirmed Smith's conversion from anarchy-spouting rabble-rouser to apostate. Total abandon, indeed – of everything she'd represented. Describing Smith as existing in 'a very naïve, very American cocoon', a disappointed Julie Burchill concluded, 'Is this the blandest record in the world?' Even Sandy Robertson, Smith's most loyal supporter in the increasingly antagonistic British press, was politely apologetic. 'The best is yet to come,' he declared unconvincingly. Quotes from Rimbaud and Genet were included on the album sleeve as if nothing had changed. But everything had.

Robertson had one last meeting with the band as part of the promotional push for that final, ignominious *Wave*. It didn't go well. 'Eighteen months ago, I'd have said that the Patti Smith Group were potentially one of the finest rock groups on the planet,' he declared. Now he regarded the band as hypocrites, carped at Smith's 'art' status and showed exasperation at Lenny Kaye's snobbish attitude and undying loyalty. He saved the sucker punch till last. The group had even developed a taste for the kind of jackets that Sting would wear. He had been, he wrote with genuine regret, 'their last true supporter in the UK press. And I'm sad about that.'

Like the generation of true believers who'd come of age with *Horses*, Robertson didn't have to wait long to be put out of his misery. The Patti Smith Group's most recent performances had been pallid affairs marked by fatigue both on stage and in the stalls. Smith herself had grown tired of the constant touring. The *coup de grâce* came in September 1979 when riots broke out at two stadium gigs in Bologna and Florence, Italy. At the first, Smith prayed as the band members were locked behind a gate backstage. In Florence, as the US flag was raised, as had been the custom, during the last song,

Smith played some improvised piano over a recording of one of the Pope's speeches. Whether the crowd was more affronted by the perceived message of sacrilege or at the sight of the imperial flag is difficult to ascertain. Perhaps it was the vainglorious changing of the words to 'Gloria' – a song that had been dropped from the set for some time – to 'Jesus died for somebody's sins – why not mine?' It was 10 September 1979, and the Patti Smith Group had played its final show.

Patti Smith retreated into the arms of Fred 'Sonic' Smith, her lover since March 1977 and the inspiration for 'Frederick', the soft-focus first single from *Wave*. Tall, quiet and with crooked teeth, Fred inspired a new rapture in Patti. Her love for him now eclipsed her feelings for the band – and her career. The pair married on 1 March 1980, and two years later Smith gave birth to the first of their two children. She threw herself into a life of domesticity on the outskirts of Detroit with all of the enthusiasm she'd shown for rock'n'roll in the mid-seventies. Just as Arthur Rimbaud had done a century earlier, she had opted for early retirement. Performing had robbed her of all her energy, and she was no longer willing to make that sacrifice. Besides, she later admitted, she had felt 'extremely false being on stage'. It was, she said, 'an honourable leave'.

Epilogue

SATURDAY, 25 June 2005, the Royal Festival Hall. Patti Smith is back in London, scene of those two triumphant Roundhouse shows back in May 1976, and performing *Horses* in its entirety. It was confirmation – as if any were needed – that the record, like the Beach Boys' *Pet Sounds* and Love's *Forever Changes*, was a rock'n'roll evergreen, a staple of those '100 Rock Albums You Must Own' polls that pop up with yawning regularity. But where Brian Wilson and Arthur Lee had recently recreated their career-defining albums in concert as ends in themselves, Smith embedded her *Horses* show in a programme of events that wide-screened the magnitude of the original record.

Few other rock'n'roll records would have justified such treatment. But *Horses* was always more than just a rock'n'roll album. It was an invitation into an entire way of life where music and aesthetics were inextricably woven into the fabric of lived experience. It was a way of life, the artist's way, which made its return as part of an extraordinarily dynamic and expansive Meltdown Festival all the more appropriate.

Patti Smith was the 13th curator of Meltdown, a pioneering and unique programme of events designed to make full use of the South Bank Centre's range of facilities. Previous incumbents, including Nick Cave, David Bowie, Scott Walker, John Peel and Morrissey, had commissioned spectacular and diverse programmes. But, according to Glenn Max, who coordinated the project, Smith's was 'perhaps the most self-referential Meltdown there's been'.

If that makes the event sound like a grand exercise in narcissism, well, it was – and for all the right reasons. A smorgasbord of pop, poetry, politics, cinema and literature, Smith's Meltdown was a celebration of an alternative tradition where all roads led invariably to *Horses*, the inspirations that lay behind it and the imprint it has left.

It was a remarkable restatement of intent, for when Smith took her 'honourable leave' in 1980, it was as much to regain a sense of artistic purity. As impressive as *Radio Ethiopia* and *Easter* had been, in their different ways, her insurrectionary rhetoric could not mask the fact that she, like so many before her, had been consumed by rock stardom. Retirement allowed her to re-engage with the wider palette of creative endeavour, to which she soon added motherhood, throwing herself into it with all the passion she had previously reserved for her art.

She had returned in 1988 with *Dream of Life*, a title likely inspired by a line from Shelley's 'Adonais', the poem read by Jagger at the Stones' 5 July 1969 concert in Hyde Park as a eulogy for the late Brian Jones. A further four albums followed, *Gone Again, Peace and Noise, Gung Ho* and *Trampin'*, though none had anything like the impact of *Horses*. Nor could they hope to. But their presence did reveal Smith as a maverick whose work invariably followed its own path, even in a post-Live Aid world where spectacle was all, and any sense of rebellion had been quietened by a complicit acceptance that the culture industries were primarily about money, marketing and massaging ever more preposterous egos.

Though undeniably bourgeois in its establishment, art-house setting, Smith's Meltdown was a riposte to all that. That 30 years had passed during which time Smith had endured greater success and greater tragedy in her life than she could ever have expected only underlined the matchlessness of her grand vision – which seemed positively hallucinatory compared with the skeletal aspirations of those who had followed in her wake.

Meltdown was a celebration of art and life, a commemoration to fallen idols and a showcase to rising stars. It was also a testament to Smith's resolve, and her unquenchable thirst to explore the creative impulse, that had been shaken to its bones during the intervening years. She had lost many friends, lovers and fellow travellers along the way. On 9 September 1989, Robert Mapplethorpe, the photographer who had done so much to imprint her image on the minds of an entire generation, had died. Richard Sohl, who had been reunited with Smith on *Dream of Life*, passed away the following year. On 11 November 1994, she lost her husband Fred Smith, just weeks before the death of her brother Todd.

She had turned once again to music and to Electric

Ladyland, where she recorded a sixth studio album, *Gone Again*. A noisier, mournful and necessarily cathartic collection, the album also paid tribute to the nineties' most tragic rock'n'roll suicide, Nirvana frontman Kurt Cobain. Among those who had lined up to support her, including Tom Verlaine and John Cale, was the saintly voiced Jeff Buckley, himself the victim of a tragic accident less than two years later.

The loss of so many friends and inspirational figures in such a short time had driven Smith back to the stage. Touring in 1995 under the banner 'Paradise Lost', she cut an often forlorn, grief-stricken figure as she supported Dylan, and turned up to speak at tribute shows for Fred Smith, Jack Kerouac, Jean Genet and Antonin Artaud. But art had saved her as a teenager; it would do so again.

* * *

When she walked into the press conference for the Meltdown Festival on 14 June 2005, Smith was jetlagged just as she had been back in October 1976. But this time there were no flying sandwiches or bile-filled responses to questions. Instead, this remarkable 59-year-old woman, who had evidently lost little of her old radicalism or belief in art as salvation, opened with a few generous lines from William Blake:

> To Mercy, Pity, Peace, and Love
> All pray in their distress;

And to these virtues of delight
Return their thankfulness.

For Mercy, Pity, Peace, and Love
Is God, our father dear,
And Mercy, Pity, Peace, and Love
Is Man, his child and care.

For Mercy has a human heart,
Pity a human face,
And Love, the human form divine,
And Peace, the human dress.

The wit and enthusiasm that had been such a tonic back in 1975 had returned, too. She explained why she wore a Ralph Nader badge in the pre-publicity photos (it was a happy accident, she said, adding that he was 'probably the most honest, intelligent man I've ever met', one who deserved a position of power), expressed her admiration for more recent female icons such as Tilda Swinton and Miranda Richardson, promised that she'd wear a dress on stage at least once and – as an echo of her old domestic-goddess role – added that she'd be ironing Jeff Beck's shirt for him before he takes the stage.

The programme of events amounted to a virtual symposium on *Horses* and Smith's metier. There were evenings celebrating the work of Brecht and Burroughs, Blake and radical French cinema, Mapplethorpe and Richard Hell. Contemporary mavericks such as the Brian Jonestown

Massacre and Antony & the Johnsons rubbed shoulders with earlier inspirations such as Television and Yoko Ono. There were radical political readings, music from non-Western traditions, children's lullabies and a grand finale, 'Songs Of Experience', that celebrated the life and art of Jimi Hendrix. It was clear that Smith's passion, her belief in the tradition she'd first tapped into as a teenager, had not dimmed one bit. Everything was shot through with a visceral rock'n'roll energy, but, as always, Patti Smith's Meltdown went way beyond that.

'I feel that this has given us an opportunity to touch upon all the aspects of our cultural voice,' she said, 'and the thing I always loved about rock'n'roll from a very young person is that rock'n'roll, whether it was Bob Dylan or Jimi Hendrix or Jim Morrison or Neil Young ... not only was it liberating in a revolutionary way, in a sexual way, but we exchanged ideas. I learned a lot about what was happening in our world, and a lot of things. We don't know how to speak for ourselves: our culture speaks for us, our artists, our war correspondents, all these people who give voice to what is happening in our world. And I think that this Meltdown, as much as we could, brings together poetry, somebody like [writer] John Lee Andersen and Richard Hell and musicians from various parts of the world, folk events, Jimi Hendrix ...' She tailed off.

It was an inspirational line-up, though it was *Horses*, performed on the penultimate night, that was the *coup de grâce*. The life-affirming record that had once so inspired Morrissey and his guitar-playing collaborator Johnny Marr, that had REM's Michael Stipe and Sonic Youth's Thurston

Moore forever proclaiming Smith as a trailblazing rock'n'roll messiah, who laid the path so that P J Harvey, Courtney Love's Hole and countless woman-fronted bands could emerge from her shadow, was being exhumed like some holy relic.

As the lights went down, those who'd spent the past three decades wondering, as Smith had done on 'Birdland', 'Am I all alone in this generation?', had their answer. They were not. The legend of *Horses* had been reclaimed, revived, reignited. Go, Johnny, go.

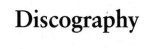

Discography

Discography

(UK catalogue numbers have been used unless otherwise stated)

SINGLES / EPS
Hey Joe (Version) / Piss Factory (1974, Mer 601; US only; reissued in p/s 1977)
Gloria / My Generation (live in Cleveland 21 January 1976) (1976 12″ Arista ARIST 135)
Ask The Angels / Time Is On My Side (live in Paris, 21 October 1976) (1977, Arista/Pathe Marconi/EMI 2C 006-98.529; France only)
Hey Joe / Radio Ethiopia (live at CBGB, 5 June 1977) (1977, 12″, Arista/Pathe Marconi/EMI 2C 052-60.133 Z; France only)
Because The Night / God Speed (1978, Arista ARIST 181)
Set Free EP (Privilege [Set Me Free], Ask The Angels, 25th Floor (Live in Paris, Easter Sunday, 1978), Babelfield (Live in London, 28 February 1978) (1978, 12", Arista ARIST 12197)
Frederick / Fire Of Unknown Origin (1979, Arista ARIST 264)

Dancing Barefoot / 5-4-3-2-1 (live in New York, 23 May 1979) (1979, Arista ARIST 281)
So You Want To Be A Rock'n'Roll Star / Frederick (live) (Arista ARIST 291)

ALBUMS

Horses Gloria (In Excelsiss Deo) / Redondo Beach / Birdland / Free Money / Kimberly / Break It Up / Land: Horses-Land Of 1,000 Dances-La Mer[de] / Elgie) (1975, Arista ARTY 122; reissued on CD in 2005 with My Generation [live] bonus track, and a second disc featuring the entire Meltdown concert, Arista/Columbia/ Legacy 82876 71198 2)

Radio Ethiopia Ask The Angels / Ain't It Strange / Poppies / Pissing In A River / Pumping [My Heart] / Distant Fingers / Radio Ethiopia / Abyssinia) (1976, Arista SPARTY 1001, with inner sleeve; reissued on CD with bonus track, Chiklets, Arista 07822 18825 2)

Easter (Till Victory / Space Monkey / Because The Night / Ghost Dance / Babeloque / Rock'n'Roll Nigger / Privilege [Set Me Free] / We Three / 25th Floor / High On Rebellion / Easter) (1978, Arista SPARTY 1043; reissued on CD with bonus track, Godspeed, Arista 07822 18826 2)

Wave (Frederick / Dancing Barefoot / So You Want To Be A Rock'n'Roll Star / Hymn / Revenge / Citizen Ship / Seven Ways Of Going / Broken Flag / Wave) (1979, Arista SPARTY 1086; reissued on CD with two bonus tracks, Fire Of Unknown Origin and 5-4-3-2-1 [live])

Dream Of Live (People Have The Power / Up There Down

There / Paths That Cross / Dream Of Life / Where Duty Calls / Going Under / Looking For You [I Was] / The Jackson Song) (1988, Arista; reissued on CD with 2 bonus tracks)

Gone Again (Gone Again / Beneath The Southern Cross / About A Boy / My Madrigal / Summer Cannibals / Dead To The World / Wing / Ravens / Wicked Messenger / Fireflies / Farewell Reel) (1996, Arista 74321 38474 2)

Peace And Noise (Waiting Underground / Whirl Away / 1949 / Spell / Don't Say Nothing / Dead City / Blue Poles / Death Singing / Memento Mori / Last Call) (1997, Arista 07822 18986 2)

Gung Ho (One Voice / Lo And Beholden / Boy Cried Wolf / Persuasion / Gone Pie / China Bird / Glitter In Their Eyes / Strange Messengers / Grateful / Upright Come / New Party / Libbie's Song / Gung Ho) (2000, Arista 07822 121624 2)

Land 1975–2002 (Dancing Barefoot / Babelogue / Rock N Roll Nigger / Gloria / Pissing In A River / Free Money / People Have The Power / Because The Night / Frederick / Summer Cannibals / Ghost Dance / Ain't It Strange / 1959 / Beneath The Southern Cross / Glitter In Their Eyes / Paths That Cross / When Doves Cry / Piss Factory / Redondo Beach [demo] / Distant Fingers [demo] / 25th Floor [live] / Come Back Little Sheba / Wander I Go / Dead City [live] / Spell [live] / Wing [live] / Boy Cried Wolf [live] / Birdland [live] / Higher Learning / Notes To The Future [live]) (2- CD compilation, 2002, Arista 07822 14208 2)

Trampin' (Jubilee / Mother Rose / Stride Of The Mind / Cartwheels / Ghandi / Trespasses / My Blakean Year / Cash / Peaceable Kingdom / Radio Baghdad / Trampin') (2004, Columbia 515215 9)

Sources

BOOKS

Antonia, Nina *The New York Dolls: Too Much Too Soon* (Omnibus Press, 1998)

Bangs, Lester Psychotic Reactions and Carburetor Dung (Minerva, 1990)

Bockris, Victor *Patti Smith* (Fourth Estate, 1998)

Johnstone, Nick *Patti Smith: A Biography* (Omnibus Press, 1997)

McCain, Gillian and McNeil, *Legs Please Kill Me: The Uncensored Oral History of Punk* (Abacus, 1997)

Reynolds, Simon and Press, Joy *The Sex Revolts: Gender, Rebellion and Rock'n'Roll* (Serpent's Tail, 1995)

Savage, Jon *England's Dreaming: Sex Pistols and Punk Rock* (Faber & Faber, 1991)

Sewall-Ruskin, Yvonne *High on Rebellion: Inside the Underground at Max's Kansas City* (Thunder's Mouth Press, 1998)

Smith, Patti *Babel* (1974–1978) (1978, Virago)

Smith, Patti *Complete 1975–2006* (Bloomsbury, 2006)
Smith, Patti *Kodak* (1972, Middle Earth, US)
Smith, Patti *Seventh Heaven* (1972, Telegraph Books, US)
Smith, Patti *WĪTT* (1973, Gotham Book Mart, US)
Solanas, Valerie *S.C.U.M. Manifesto* (AK Press, 1997)

MAGAZINES & NEWSPAPERS

Circus, Crawdaddy, Creem, Daily Telegraph, Fusion, Guardian, Independent on Sunday, Interview, Jazz & Pop, Mademoiselle, Melody Maker, Music Scene, New Musical Express, Penthouse, Record Mirror, Rock Scene, Rolling Stone, Soho News, Sounds, The Village Voice, White Stuff

WRITERS

Firstly, I'd particularly like to thank Charles Shaar Murray and Steve Lake for igniting the debate that forms the basis for this book. It was Murray's review of the album – still the most influential I've read in four decades of devouring the music press – that prompted me to buy *Horses* in the first place.

Other writers whose work, whether via interviews or critique, has proved invaluable include: Keith Altham, Chris Brazier, Julie Burchill, Gordon Burn, Scott Cohen, Caroline Coon, Giovanni Dadamo, Robert Demorest, Pete Erskine, Penny Green, Amy Gross, Allen Jones, Robin Katz, Lenny Kaye, Nick Kent, Dave Marsh, Lucy O'Brien, Simon Reynolds,

Sandy Robertson, Lisa Robinson, Susan Shapiro, Sam Shepard, Jane Suck, Nick Tosches, Paul Williams. And, of course, Patti Smith.

MISCELLANEOUS

I also consulted a wide range of sources, too numerable to specify individually, on Rimbaud and Baudelaire, Godard and Modigliani, the Rolling Stones and Jimi Hendrix, and assorted Smith-related topics.

Picture Credits

Page 1 Corbis

Page 2 (*top left*) Corbis; (*top right*) Rex Features; (*bottom*) Seated Nude (oil on canvas), Modigliani, Amedeo (1884–1920) / Koninklijk Mueseum voor Schone Kunsten, Antwerp, Belgium, Giraudon / The Bridgeman Art Library

Page 3 (*top*) Corbis; (*bottom*) Allan Tannenbaum

Page 4 (*top*) Corbis; (*middle*) Corbis; (*bottom left)* Redferns; (*bottom right*) Corbis

Page 5 (*top*) Corbis; (*bottom*) Corbis

Page 6 (*top left*) Redferns; (*top right*) Corbis; (*bottom*) Corbis

Page 7 (*top left*) Redferns; (*bottom*) Corbis

Page 8 (*top*) Corbis; (*bottom*) ArenaPAL/topfoto

Index